CW01475299

NEEDLES TO NAB

Island Seaborne Trades

Michael Langley

Front cover pictures, please see:
Top left - caption 177
Top right - caption 48
Lower left - caption 128
Lower right - caption 64

Back cover: Speed's 1627 Isle of Wight Map

About the Author -

An early interest in photography, coastal shipping and the harbours of Sussex would lead to a career in deep sea shipping with the P&O Group culminating in Ship Management. A later move to the Isle of Wight saw a return to the original interests resulting in research and publication of a number of local history style shipping books for the areas from Kent to Cornwall.

Published November 2012

ISBN 978 1 908174 33 8

© Middleton Press, 2012

Design Deborah Esher

Published by
Middleton Press
Easebourne Lane
Midhurst
West Sussex
GU29 9AZ
Tel: 01730 813169
Fax: 01730 812601
Email: info@middletonpress.co.uk
www.middletonpress.co.uk

Printed in the United Kingdom by Henry Ling Limited, at the Dorset Press, Dorchester, DT1 1HD

CONTENTS

SUMMARIES

PREFACE

Before 1800 little mobility existed amongst the Island's small populace. However by the very nature of the place considerable cross-Solent trade had thrived for centuries especially the export of agricultural produce and import of coal and general goods. The few brave souls who did cross the Solent travelled in small boats or the notorious rowing wherries, all much dependent on favourable winds and tide. The local arrival of paddle steamers from around 1820, construction of piers and railways from the 1840s onward would set the pattern for the future. The intention of this book is to examine the ships, trades and industries served during the 19th and 20th centuries.

Images note - a number of the illustrations have appeared before but are included for their overall rarity value to highlight certain seldom photographed vessels, locations and trades.

GLOSSARY & ABBREVIATIONS

SS Steam Ship
PS Paddle steamer
TS Training Ship
MV Motor Vessel
MT Motor Tanker
MT Motor Tug
THV Trinity House Vessel
MTB Twin Screw Motor Barge

Tonnages:
Gross Registered Tonnage, abbr. grt; g, volumetric measure of all enclosed space applied to all ships. 100cu.ft. = 1 gross ton. Indicator of a ship's overall physical size.

Net Registered Tonnage, abbr. nrt, n, sometimes referred to as just registered tonnage. Derivation from sailing ship days in the wine trade when a 'tun'* implied a wine barrel of 252 gallons capacity. The number of such barrels gave an indication of carrying volume. * Wine tun decreed to be of 252 gallons by Act in 1423.

Deadweight Tonnage, abbr. dwt, d, the actual weight carrying capacity of the ship in tons, including fuel, water, stores etc, plus cargo.

Tons 'burthen' or 'burden' were statements of deadweight used for cargo ships in the 17th and 18th centuries.

Scantlings:
Set of standard dimensions for parts used in construction in ship building.

Knots/ kts:
Speed in nautical miles (6,080ft) per hour.

Spring Tides:
Fortnightly periods of greater tidal range – 'higher' high water and 'lower' low water.

Neap Tides:
Intervening periods of lesser tidal range – 'lower' high water and 'higher' low water.

Littoral Drift:
The eastward movement of shingle along the Channel shoreline.

Some early commodity measures – volumetric:
Heaped or dry, ie. in the corn trade:
One Chaldron = 36 Bushels = 12 sacks
[1.3 m3 or 1300 litres modern, or 35.32cu.ft.]
Chaldron also deemed to be approximately 28cwt. (hundred weights)
One Bushel = 4 Pecks or 8 Gallons.
One Sack = 3 Bushels or 24 Gallons
One Quarter = 28 lbs or 12.7 Kilos
Four Quarters = 1 Cwt. or 50.8Kilos
Twenty Hundredweight = 1 Ton (Imperial)

Timber imports:
A common traditional measure was the Petrograd Standard consisting of 120 pieces equalling 165 cu.ft.. As an approximate guide depending on timber density one standard equalled 2.5 – 3 tons, prior to the later metrication of the trade.

DEFINITIONS

Sailing Vessel Types:

Smack: Historical term describing small single masted trading or fishing vessels.

Sloop: As above with fore and aft rig – one head sail, gaff rigged.

Cutter: As above but with two headsails and a running bowsprit, also gaff rigged.

Hoy: Old type of single masted heavily built trading vessel for carrying goods and passengers out to ships at anchor or on coastwise voyages. The type existed from around 1500 until the 1800s.

Lugger: Two or three masted vessels with four cornered sails used for fishing. The central mast was made redundant by the mid 1800s. Large fast versions of luggers were used by the Royal Navy, Smugglers and the Revenue Service!

Yawl: Small fishing or trading vessel whose tiny mizzen mast was stepped abaft the rudder post. Gaff rigged. Not so common.

Ketch: Larger fishing and trading types with larger mizzen mast stepped ahead of the rudder post. Gaff rigged, very common type.

Schooner: Trading vessel with two, three or more masts fore and aft rigged. often carried one or two square topsails on the foremast.

Brig: Two masted square rigged trading vessel.

Snow: As per the brig but with an additional small mast immediately abaft the mainmast. It carried the 'spanker' sail only.

Brigantine: As per the brig but square rigged on the foremast only, and fore and aft rigged on the mainmast. This was more economic on manpower.

Barque: Larger square rigged sailing ship. If square rigged on all masts was known as a 'full rigged ship'.

Barquentine: Square rigged on foremast only, fore and aft sails on other masts.

Spritsail Barge: Shallow draughted coastal and esturial vessels rigged with a large spar extending from near the base of the mainmast (and sometimes the mizzen), to the upper outer corner of the sail.
Thames and Medway sailing barges are the best known of the type.

Wherry: Light, shallow rowing boats for carrying passengers short distances.

Sea Coal: arch. Originally described coal brought South from Newcastle.

tpa: tons per annum

INTRODUCTION

Rising sea levels following the last ice age caused England's final land bridge to mainland Europe to be severed. Just a few thousand years ago the west to east flowing Solent River would be lost beneath the deepening sea ingress and the Isle of Wight formed. Further sea level rise, coastal erosion and river siltation from the land would produce the basic diamond shaped island we see today.

Early sea-going vessels were tiny and doubtless made use of all the local creeks, rivers and beaches when conditions allowed. The Island's geographical position jutting out into the Channel rendered it vital for fortification against impending invaders from elsewhere in Europe. By 1800 simple single masted sailing vessels such as smacks, cutters and sloops had been joined by ketches, brigs, barques, schooners and sailing barges, all variously involved in cross-Solent and longer distance trades.

Steamships appeared locally from around 1820 preceding the arrival of the railways in the 1840s-1860s period. The first Island pier, timber constructed, appeared in 1814 at Ryde but would soon be rebuilt with cast iron supports and many other piers shortly opened for business. Locally, industrial growth coincided with the 1845 arrival of Queen Victoria and Prince Albert who chose Osborne House at East Cowes as the family retreat. Princess Victoria had stayed at Norris Castle in 1831 with her mother.

The railways arrived here in 1862 thereby greatly increasing the demand for and ability to shift coal around the Island. Gasworks proliferated from around 1820 spreading to most Island towns, and from 1900 a similar spread of local electricity generation works arrived. All required some form of imported fuel. As demand rose ships grew larger and facilities expanded to efficiently and safely accommodate them. Wharves in sheltered harbours posed much less of an insurance risk to ship and cargo owners in comparison to unloading on open beaches.

Victorian railways with service reliability gave the general populace unheard of mobility and this would soon lead to the tripper, excursion and holiday market development. A number of companies became involved in the goods and luggage transit business to and from the mainland. Shepard Brothers, and Crouchers, both Newport based firms, operated from the early 1800s carrying any cargo on offer. Carter Paterson, Curtiss & Sons and Chaplins were also involved in cross-Solent goods shipment, along with Pickfords who operated 'tow-boats' as did the railway companies for the carriage of horses, livestock, vans, carts and small commercial vehicles whose numbers steadily grew in the early 20th century. Chaplins was a 'rail carrier' company based at Ryde Esplanade.

The Island wide distribution of goods (and some passengers too) in the pre-motor vehicle era had been undertaken by a large group of specialist tradesmen known as the carriers. They would collect goods from wherever required and ran regular services with their horses and carts or vans to even the smallest outlying hamlets in rural Wight, perhaps on just a couple of days per week, but daily where demand existed. Steam wagons also delivered Island wide with larger items or bulk goods. From around WW1 small petrol driven lorries and vans started to take over such duties and the early motor bus and charabanc services developed to the detriment and ultimate near demise of the local railways.

Motor powered vessels also multiplied from around the time of WW1 and they would ultimately supercede the steamers and the remaining traditional sailing ships still involved in cross-Solent trade. From 1927 the first tentative advance into roll-on, roll-off ferry operation commenced but it would nevertheless take a further fifty years to completely eliminate the general purpose cargo barge trade. By the 1970s Island generation of gas and electricity had been replaced by under sea connections to the mainland with pipelines and cables. North Sea gas ensured the closure nationally of all coal fired gas plants. The national grid system would similarly provide a uniform electric power supply from whatever generation source was available, to all.

Other once important Island industries such as salt manufacturing, beer brewing, corn/flour milling, cement manufacture, ship and boat building and flying boat construction are all examined within. Today specialist boat building, defence electronic systems and aviation support manufacturing are the major players in the Island's industrial economy.

Map No.1 ISLE OF WIGHT (general)

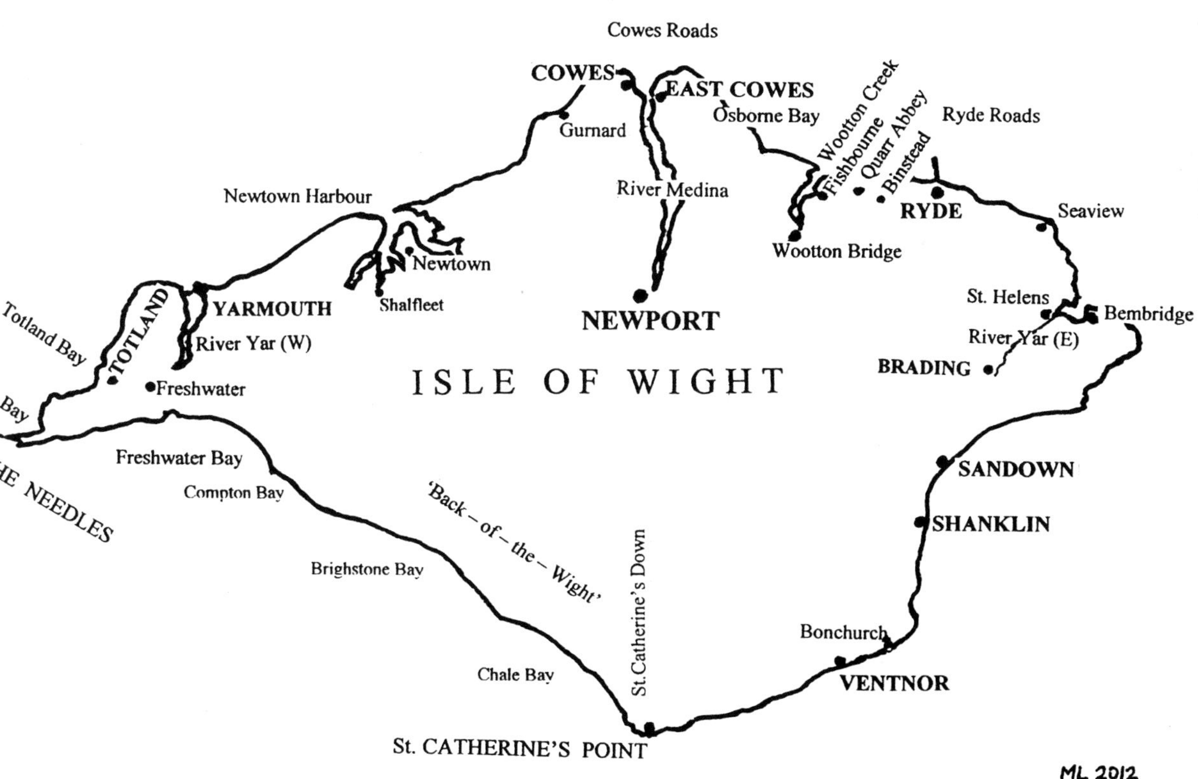

1. The first Needles Lighthouse

This delightful image is seen courtesy of Carisbrooke Castle Museum. The tower was situated in an elevated position overlooking the Needles. The chalk ridge once continued to the Dorset coast before the Island's creation by rising sea levels. Built in 1785 on the cliff summit above the rocks, the light would have been of little use to navigation in 'fog, mist, falling snow, heavy rainstorms, or any other condition similarly restricting visibility' - to quote the ruling Regulations for the Prevention of Collisions at Sea'. The present light marking the outer extremity of the Needles was built in 1859. In accordance with Trinity House's modernisation and automation of all lights, it is now remotely controlled without permanent keepers. A helicopter platform atop now forms the access for visiting maintenance staff.

2. The modern Lighthouse →

Seen from the deck of PS *WAVERLEY* in 1997 the helicopter platform is clearly visible and the location of the original cliff top tower lay where the lookout can be seen top right.

3. SS GURNARD →

Provision of a pilotage service for incoming and departing ships has long been another very important function for Trinity House. In this photograph one of the last of the steam pilot cutters is seen on station with her transfer launch approaching. This 342grt 1932 built vessel would remain on station for a week at a time acting as accommodation for outbound ship pilots awaiting an incoming vessel. By the 1960s such functions were rendered unnecessary as the service switched to fast shore based motorised pilot launches, putting to sea as and when required.

4. PS BOURNEMOUTH QUEEN at Totland Pier

Built at Troon in 1908 this 353grt paddle steamer entered service specifically as an excursion vessel in the Solent area. The postcard image shows the ship in original form during the 1930s. On returning to Red Funnel after WW2 service the ship was modified and updated with an enclosed wheelhouse and a more modern, better proportioned, funnel. She sailed on until 1957. Totland Pier opened for business in 1880 and although out of use for some years now, it still stands.

5. PS EMBASSY →

Once a stalwart of the joint LB&SC Railway and L&SW Railway Portsmouth – Ryde Pier service, which she worked as *Duchess of Norfolk*, this 381grt paddler dating from 1911 moved on to Weymouth and the excursion fleet of Cosens Ltd in 1937. Many folk still remember her trips in the Weymouth, Swanage, Bournemouth and Isle of Wight areas which lasted until 1967 and the ship's demise at Continental breakers. An end of an era indeed.

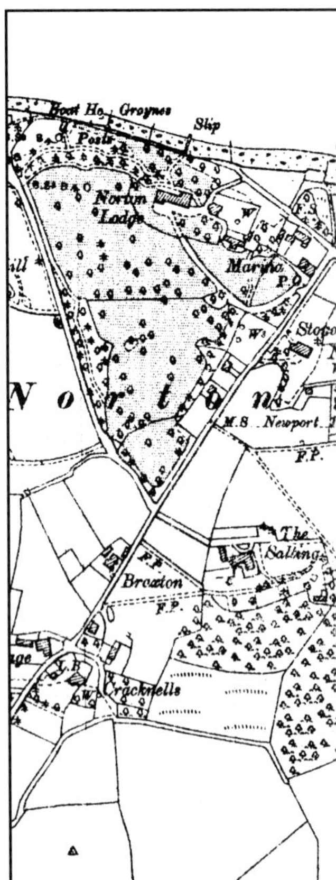

Map No.2 Yarmouth Harbour

(1) The Sand House by Yar Bridge
(2) Yarmouth Mill (corn)
(3) West Wight Gasworks, Salterns.

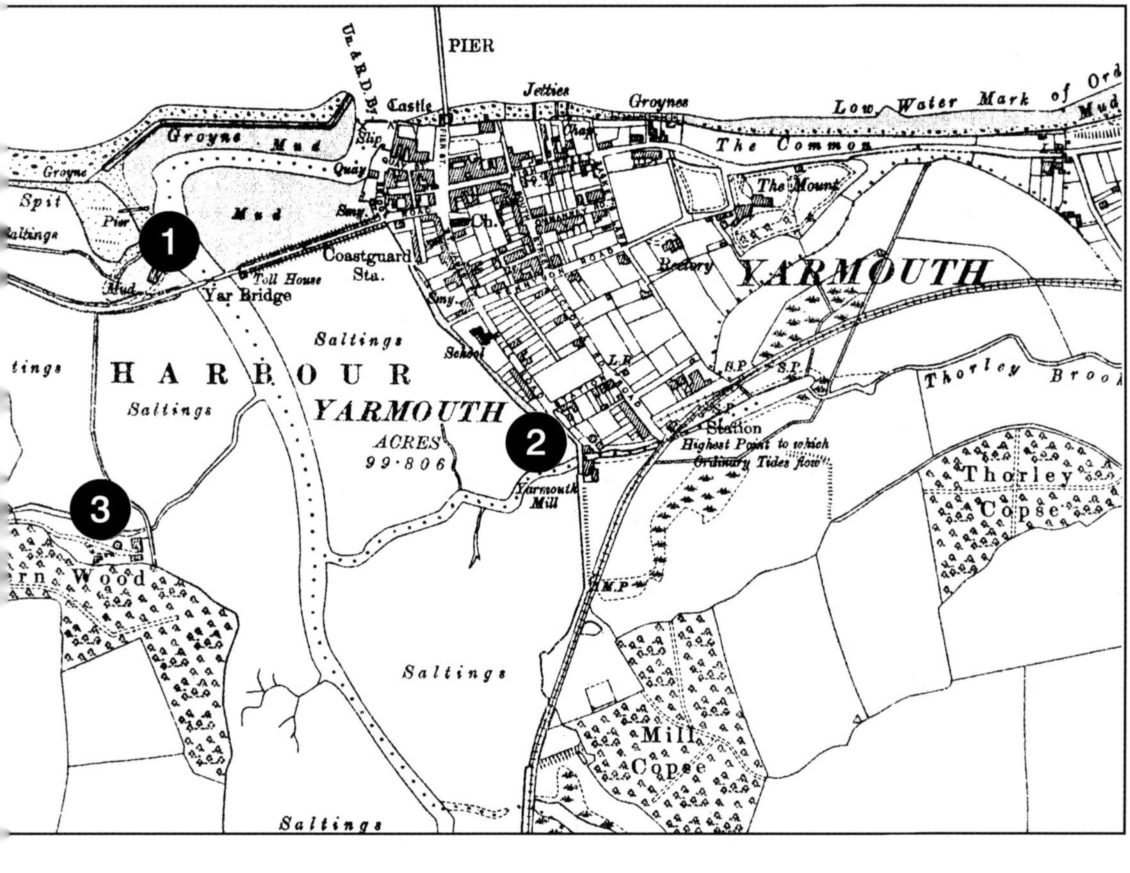

PIER
Ur. & R.D. By.
Castle
Jetties
Groynes
Low Water Mark of Ord
Mud
Groyne
Mud
Slip
Quay
Groyne
Spit
Saltings
Pier
Mud
Smy.
The Common
The Mount
Ch.
Coastguard
Sta.
Rectory
YARMOUTH
Toll House
Yar Bridge
Mud
1
Saltings
Smy.
School
L.B.
S.P.
S.P.
HARBOUR
Saltings
YARMOUTH
ACRES
99·806
2
Yarmouth
Mill
Station
Highest Point to which
Ordinary Tides flow
Thorley Brook
Thorley
Copse
3
Wood
M.P.
Saltings
Mill
Copse
Saltings

6. The River Yar

One of the many magnificent Brannon family engravings of IOW scenes, this view has much of interest worthy of close observation. It dates from 1860 and is remarkably accurate considering it is 'taken' from an imaginery position out over the sea! Yarmouth Harbour had been enclosed by a breakwater in the 1840s. Of course the hills in the image are disproportionately high, together with the masts of the relatively small trading vessels, in relation to Yarmouth church tower. Centrally the new 1860 bridge has appeared across the Yar and the Sand House lies exactly as it does today. Craft visible include two or three trading vessels, two of which are underway with square topsails set. Smaller local craft are scattered about the place. Today, the modern car ferry terminal abuts Yarmouth Castle, far left. Distant, between the tall masted vessels, Yarmouth Mill can be seen.

7. Yarmouth, ships at the Quay, c1869 →

The toll bridge, centre background, had been there for barely ten years, but the Sand House nearby more likely had already put in a century. In this fine study of the harbour there are several ketch barge traders scattered about in this low water scene and dredging looks to be increasingly necessary. The old brig with lower yards 'cockbilled' to keep them clear of other craft alongside, was probably the regular North-east coast collier of the day at Yarmouth. Berthed nearest to the camera is an early paddle steamer with some basic seating around the after deck. Evidently she was conned from a flimsy looking plank 'bridge' between the paddle boxes yet steered from a large wheel just visible right aft. The Southampton and Isle of Wight Steam Packet Company were running services in the area at the time, and this vessel is thought to be PS *Emerald*, 43grt, and of 32hp - an early Red Funnel steamer.

Drawn & Engraved by G. Brannon
Published by the Engr. Wotton I.W. May 20, 1860
THE RIVER YAR, I.W.
EXPLANATION. — The beautiful Village of NORTON, occupies the foreground of the right Bank of the River, containing several genteel Residences, of which the most prominent are The Marina, & Norton Lodge, (both on the Beach), & West Cliff, above the latter as the eye advances; Freshwater Church, with part of the Village; the Seat called Farringford; & the Beacon on High Down, which is the most elevated portion of the Freshwater range. On the left stands the Town of YARMOUTH: in the distance Afton Manor House, &c. The singular triangular Object in the River marks a dangerous Reef of sunken Rocks (called Fiddler's Race); & the insulated Building beyond is a large Store for the white sand of Alum Bay.

8. RAPID ↓

The brigantine visible in this delightful postcard image belonged to Capt. Henry Digby of Yarmouth. *Rapid* 177grt/1861 was originally built and owned in Sussex at Shoreham, rigged as a brig. Later she became Yarmouth's last regular domestic coal boat and she was re-rigged as a brigantine. The coal cargoes would have been of the order of 200 tons per trip from Hartlepool to Yarmouth's quay bunkers. The image probably dates from about 1905 and the ship is riding high awaiting her next trip North. A smaller topsail schooner lies inboard with a stout gang plank to the quay for wheelbarrow unloading of cargo. Yarmouth's domestic coal trade by sea is said to have ceased around 1907. The old ship sailed on until 1919 for London owners still in the coal trade when she was lost in ballast in the Thames Estuary, en route from London to the Tyne.

9. The Gasworks coal delivered

The steam coaster seen here has just discharged her cargo of coal at the Salterns (West Wight) Gasworks site on the west bank of the Yar at Norton. She is about to pass out through the opened Yar bridge and proceed to sea. Although the ship's port of registry, London, can be made out, the exact name cannot be verified. She is thought to be one of a standard series of small steam coasters built around 1920 for Walford Lines of London. All had 'Jolly' names such as *Jolly Frank*, *Helen, Marie*, etc. The fleet grew quite large in the 1920s and 1930s but dwindled rapidly thereafter just leaving a couple of small motor coasters trading into the 1960s. The image is believed to date from c1920. The ship carried some 350-400 tons of cargo.

10. MT JUMSEY and tow-boat →

Before 1927 (on the Portsmouth-Ryde route) and 1938 (Lymington-Yarmouth) motor cars, lorries, farm vehicles and livestock had to be transported across the Solent by way of tow-boats. These were originally wooden constructed barges with one drop end allowing access. They were unpowered craft and had to be towed either by the regular paddle steamers or designated tugs from slipway to slipway. Despite her large funnel the little Dutch built tug *Jumsey*, 30grt/1928, of 70hp was in fact a motor vessel. She is seen here arriving at Yarmouth in the 1930s with one quite large tow-boat. A single saloon car is sharing the trip with a lorry carrying a large tank or boiler ready for unloading. *Jumsey* belonged to the James Dredging, Towing and Transportation Company of London. She was still hard at work in the 1960s spotted by your author when she was attending dredging operations at Newhaven.

11. MV LYMINGTON →

The entry into service in 1938 of this fine purpose built double-ended passenger and vehicle ferry marked a giant leap forward for the Lymington-Yarmouth route. The Southern Railway were surprisingly great innovators and *Lymington* could carry some 400 passengers and 16 cars per trip. She was the first British ferry to have the advanced Voith-Schneider directional propulsion system fitted. The ship was very successful and remained on the route until 1973. Later she carried two separate pole masts for the navigation lights and a radar installation. British Railways, successors to the Southern, closed the Newport to Yarmouth and Freshwater railway line in 1953.

HOLIDAY COMFORT

is assured by sending your Luggage in advance. Carter Paterson will arrange this for you to any place.

CARTER PATERSON & Co. LTD.

EXPRESS CARRIERS LONDON

12. PS SUSSEX QUEEN (ex FRESHWATER)

The last paddler to work the Lymington-Yarmouth route had been the Southern Railway's *Freshwater* 264grt/1927, a product of Samuel White's Shipyard at Cowes. By 1959 this attractive little steamer became redundant as newer motor car ferries came into service. At one time the ship was 'earmarked' for possible preservation and in view of her manageable size and modernity compared to most paddlers remaining at the time, she would have made an excellent candidate. She made a brief appearance on the Sussex coast as *Sussex Queen* in the 1960 season, and in Dorset for the 1961 season as *Swanage Queen*. Scrapping occurred shortly thereafter.

13. MV FRESHWATER →

Built in 1959 the second *Freshwater* 350grt worked on the Lymington route with the Lymington, and Farringford of 1947, until the introduction of the three 'C' class ferries from 1973. In this photograph taken in 1971 Yarmouth's slipway looks very basic – note the large baulks of timber laying about the place – these would be positioned against the lip of the ferry's ramp to ease the passage of wheels on or off. The sharp eyed may just be able to make out far distant right, the bridge and funnel of the MV *Bournemouth Queen* – that ship was the ex Scarborough excursion vessel *Coronia* 225grt of 1935. She came South to work locally for Croson & Co. of Poole.

14. MV BALMORAL ↓

Seen berthing at Yarmouth pier in June 2004 is the preserved ex Red Funnel ferry *Balmoral* 688grt/1949. Built by Thorneycrofts of Southampton for the regular Cowes to Southampton passenger service the vessel would remain to see the end of Red Funnel's interest in the dwindling excursion trade locally in 1968. She later passed to P. & A. Campbell for operations in the Bristol Channel and since 1985 has worked as a fund raising consort to the preserved steam paddler *Waverley*. Both ships still make regular summer appearances along the South Coast. The dazzling white shape (lower right) is part of the then newly restored Yarmouth Pier woodwork. The ship may be seen later in the book in her original Red Funnel livery.

15. Yarmouth's Sand House

The 'L' shaped stone building seen in this 2010 photograph has stood for a very long time indeed. (It can also be seen in the Nos.6 & 7 images). In the early 1800s sand was brought to Yarmouth from Alum Bay by horse and cart, and probably small vessels, in order to consolidate ship loads for export to Runcorn. Here the plate glass industry was expanding although the white sand also went to other mainland areas to various porcelain manufacturers. It seems that the discovery of an even finer sand in France c1851 led to the demise of Yarmouth's export trade. However, Alum Bay coloured sands are as popular as ever with the tourists seeking local souvenirs. Today, the Sand House lies within the harbour boatyard.

16. Yarmouth swing bridge →

The ever increasing weight, size and volume of modern vehicular traffic did not bode well for the old 1860 bridge across the Yar. After not inconsiderable prevarication and delay it was finally replaced by this attractive modern version as recently as 1987. It opens at regular times for the yachts to percolate upstream, and to the Salterns Boatyard, site of the old West Wight Gasworks.

17. Yarmouth Mill →

An embankment was built as early as 1664 but the mill building seen in this 2010 photograph dates from 1793. Originally it would have been powered by way of the extensive head waters of the Thorley Brook and its tidal range. Later the mill had steam power. Seaborne cargoes of grain and flour were brought to and from the mill by small local trading ketches and barges until closure around 1905. The building was subsequently converted to residential use.

WIGHTlink
Isle of Wight Ferries
Cenwulf

Lifeboats

← 18. CENWULF

In late Wightlink livery here we see one of the class of 1973 work horses of the Lymington-Yarmouth route arriving in the latter port, in 2003. *Cenwulf* 761grt had replaced the earlier *Lymington* and her own replacement would come along in 2009 in the form of the *Wight Sky* class of ship.

← 19. WIGHT LIGHT and Yarmouth's lifeboat 2010

Two generations of car ferries have come and gone since the early *Lymington* already described, and *Farringford* of 1947. The MV *Freshwater* appeared in 1959 and similar vessels *Camber Queen* and *Fishbourne (2)* operated on the Portsmouth-Fishbourne route. Between 1969 and 1973 the next new class arrived in the form of *Cuthred,Cenwulf, Cenred* and *Caedmon*. The latter transferred to the Western Solent in 1983 when she had become surplus on the Portsmouth route. The newest trio of ferries for the Yarmouth route started to appear in 2009 when the 'Wight' class came into service. These vessels are named *Wight Light, Wight Sky* and *Wight Sun*. In the 2010 photograph Wight Light is at the berth whilst Yarmouth's current fine lifeboat the *RNLI Eric and Susan Hiscock* – named after local famous yachtsmen – sits in its own protected berth awaiting the next 'shout'.

20. WIGHT SKY

Seen departing Yarmouth in 2009, one of the newest trio sets off for Lymington. A feature not seen before is the central hydraulically raised 'garage deck' which is used without ramps lifts completely within an upper deck recess surrounded by the passenger accommodation area. A smaller traditional ramped deck is fitted to one side. These ships are still of necessity fitted with separate side entrances for foot passenger access at Yarmouth, and at Lymington Pier for the railway customers.

21. THE MILLER

Lying quietly to her anchor off Bouldnor, just east of Yarmouth in 2003 is the little motor barge *The Miller* 118grt/1932. A typical small esturial type motor coaster of her day, she was built for E. Marriage & Sons Ltd, of East Mills, Colchester. Now in private hands the little ship looks in fine fettle and is based in the West Country. Some additional accommodation has been constructed in the form of a deckhouse just forward of the wheelhouse base.

22. STADT AMSTERDAM

Another interesting vessel making use of Bouldnor's sheltered anchorage this time in 2004 is the magnificent Dutch sail training ship *Stadt Amsterdam*. She is a modern 'full rigged ship' implying that yards and square sails are carried on each mast. If the after or mizzen mast had been fore and aft rigged she would have been classed as a three masted barque.

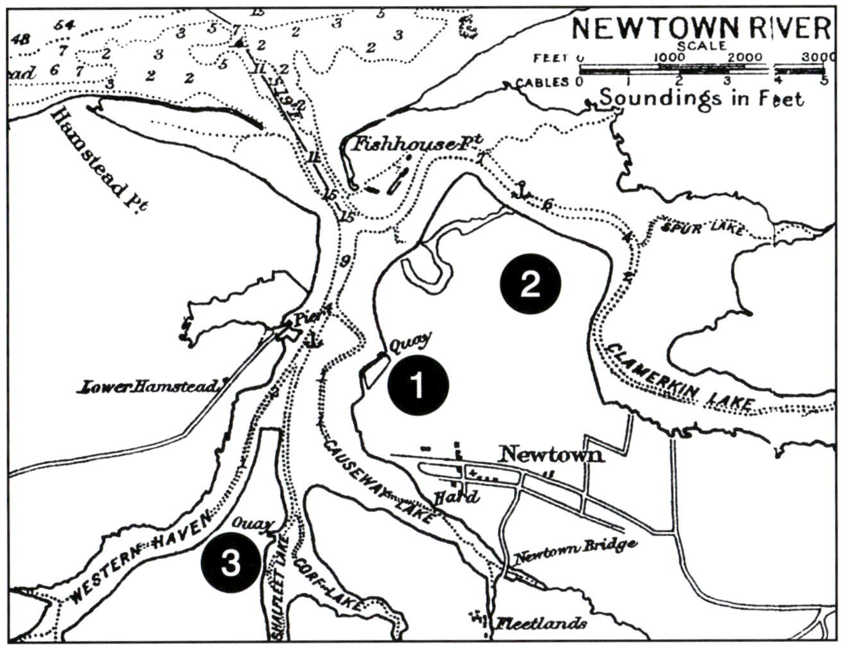

Map No. 3
Newtown Harbour

(1) Newtown Quay and saltpans
(2) Area reclaimed in the 18th Century, inundated in 1954
(3) Shalfleet Quay.

23. Newtown's historic Coat of Arms

Before describing this, a brief history of Newtown is essential. Although a settlement probably existed long before, Newtown's prominence rose in the mid 12th Century when the Bishop of Winchester established a 'Free Town' known as Francheville. It became important for salt production and export to the mainland, also for oyster fisheries. Before the 1377 French invasion a reported five hundred souls were employed here in maritime trades and activities. The harbour, still extensive today, developed from a tributary to the great Solent River which flowed from west to east before the Island's final formation. Newtown's proximity to the Beaulieu River enhanced its value as a safe crossing place. The harbour was said to be able to accommodate fifty vessels of 500 tons at one time. After the sacking of the town by the French it seems that an almost terminal decline set in and by 1600 only eleven houses remained in the Parish. In 1831 just sixty eight souls dwelled hereabouts. In 1916 the last public house closed for ever and the fine seal seen in the photograph adorns the old pub wall. The simple ship design on the seal shows a single square sailed vessel with fore and aft fighting 'castles', little different in construction to Viking types except for the castles.

24. Shalfleet Quay, Newtown Harbour

On a sunny November day in 2010 the harbour workboats rest at their berth. Shalfleet Quay once saw cargoes of corn for shipment and the import of coal and slate for local use. Warehouses stood adjacent to the quay which was particularly busy in the 18th and 19th centuries. Today, Newtown Harbour is a splendid quiet nature reserve under the care of the National Trust.

25. Newtown Quay →

Saltworks are believed to have been sited at Newtown since Norman times, the shallower parts of the harbour affording easy construction for large evaporating saltpans. Salt collected would be further treated in a nearby boiler house. There were no less than seven saltworks at one time, diminishing to three by 1880. The salt was shipped out from the quay close to what is now known as the 'black hut'. The photograph dates from 2010.

26. Gurnard Luck →

About four miles to the north-east of Newtown lies the tiny inlet known as Gurnard Luck. This miniscule creek is thought to have once extended, and been navigable much further inland. Lepe on the Hampshire coast is merely 2.5 miles distant and this would have made Gurnard an important Solent crossing point long ago, especially before Cowes developed. A Roman villa is believed to have been lost to the sea in this area.

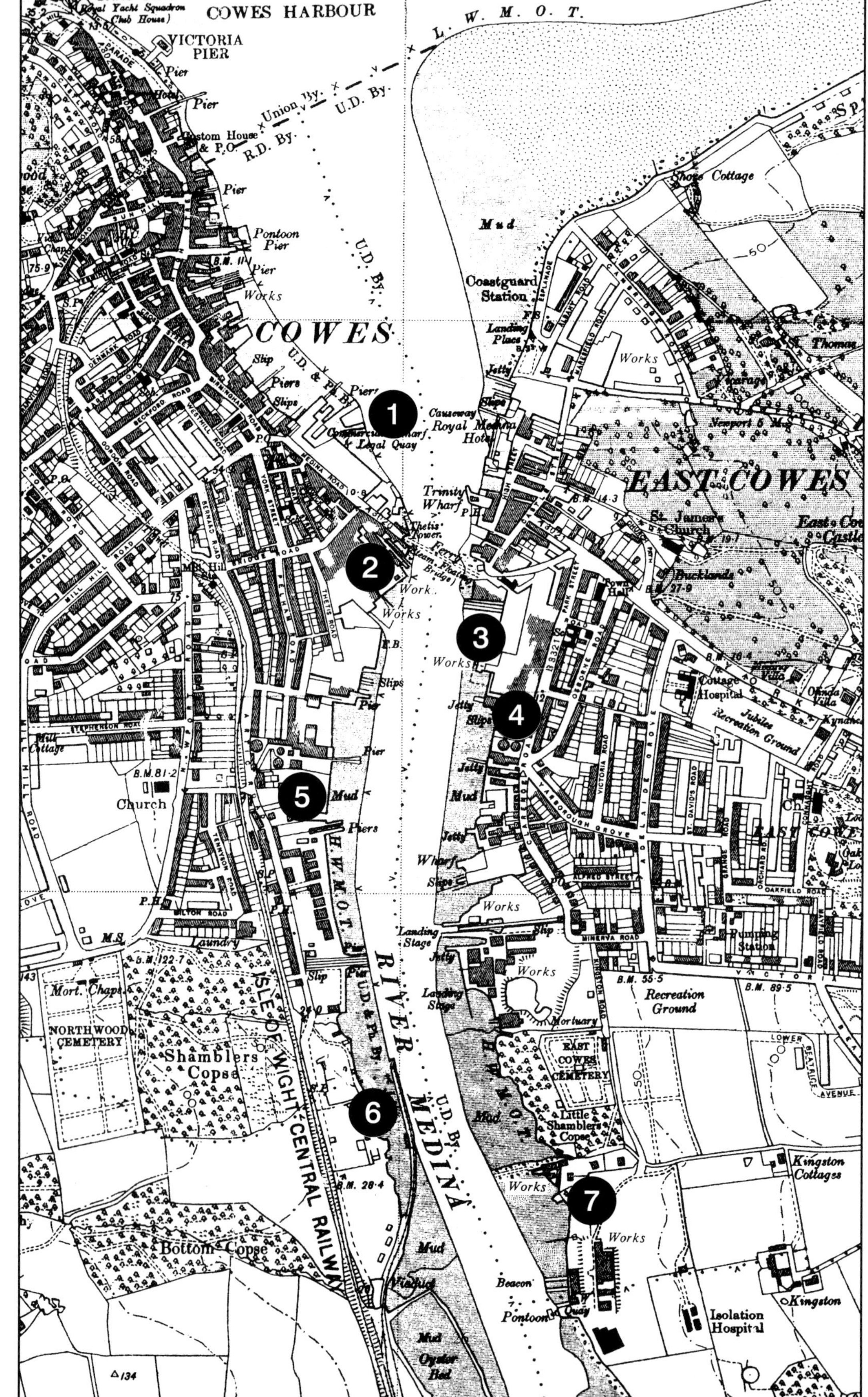

COWES HARBOUR
VICTORIA PIER
COWES
EAST COWES
RIVER MEDINA
ISLE OF WIGHT CENTRAL RAILWAY
NORTHWOOD CEMETERY
Shamblers Copse
Bottom Copse
EAST COWES CEMETERY
Little Shamblers Copse
Isolation Hospital
Kingston
Kingston Cottages
Recreation Ground
Jubilee Recreation Ground
Cottage Hospital
Coastguard Station
Royal Medina Hotel
Commercial Wharf & Legal Quay
Trinity Wharf
Floating Bridge
Mud
Mud Oyster Bed
1
2
3
4
5
6
7

← Map No. 4 Cowes and the River Medina prior to 1923

(1) General goods wharves and piers
(2) J. Samuel White's fitting out quays
(3) J. Samuel White's Falcon Shipyard, East Cowes
(4) East Cowes Gasworks, Clarence Road
(5) West Cowes Gasworks, Arctic Road
(6) Medina Wharf, pre Southern Railway pier arrangement
(7) Site of later Gas and Electricity Generating Stations.

27. A sailing coaster rounding Calshot (1805)

A delightful image taken from an aquatint shows a coastal trading ship rounding Calshot Spit and Castle, with the Isle of Wight faintly visible in the background. The vessel has an ornate taffrail and stern not unlike the craft (seen later in the book) unloading at Ryde Sands. There was much legal wrangling and little agreement before 1800 as to what constituted a cutter or a sloop type. Whether the craft should have a running or steeved (angled) bowsprit could not satisfactorily be settled. Today a sloop is generally deemed to carry a mainsail and one foresail. In old Royal Navy terms if it carried guns it would have been described as a cutter. A modern cutter has a mainsail and two foresails plus bowsprit. All were originally gaff rigged. The vessels shown in the image carry yards for a single large square topsail for when advantageous following wind conditions allowed.

28. Calshot Point and a Princess Flying Boat

The entrance to Southampton Water has been guarded by various fortifications and watch towers for centuries (see No.27). One industry that became very important to Cowes started as early as 1914 when the foundling Saunders-Roe Company began to construct seaplanes for WW1 military use. Continued design improvements and Company evolution would see 'SARO' develop a number of new projects including after WW2, Britain's early rocket technology, and the new hovercraft industry. The Princess Flying Boat project however, had begun in 1944 although as yet unnamed. Plans were made for two large flying boats to be placed on a London to New York service. The now familiar giant Union flag is painted on the door of the huge construction hanger which at East Cowes, with its slipway in front, appeared in 1936 in readiness

for the anticipated construction of larger flying boats. The flying boats of Imperial Airways were popular before WW2 for long haul routes and it was thought that such passenger demand would continue to increase post WW2. The ocean going passenger liners had previously had the monopoly of long distance global travel. However the war left the aviation industry proceeding in entirely another development direction. Four engined propeller planes, the subsequent arrival of jets plus the availability of newly built lengthy runways, would see a terminal lack of interest in flying boat prospects. Nevertheless three 'Princess' flying boat hulls were completed at Cowes but only one totally fitted out and air trials tested. In 1954 all three were set aside and mothballed in special cacoons. Two were towed across to Calshot Spit and the third remained at East Cowes. This last one went under tow to the River Itchen breakers in 1967. In the photograph just one is present at the Calshot lay-up site and another vanishing once essential service can be seen out on the water where two Air-Sea RAF rescue launches are awaiting action in this 1950s coastal scene.

← 29. Egypt Point Light House

In comparison to the rather grander Needles Light in the west and the Nab Tower in the east, this curious structure is rather mundane. It does, nevertheless, mark the northern tip of the Island coastline. Calshot Light Vessel opposite this site was replaced many years ago by a large navigational buoy.

← 30. A pair of Cowes ketches c1900

Seen 'ghosting' along or even moored on a calm murky day, this pair of Cowes built ketches are hoping for a breeze to proceed to sea and the mainland for the next cargo. *Lydia* 16reg./1867 and *Ellen* 18reg./1869 exhibit the very long booms and gaffs of their type. In 1872 *Lydia* traded for James Denman of Yarmouth, *Ellen* for Charles Price of Newport. By 1900, the two vessels were owned by W.T. Ansell and Shepard Bros. of Newport, respectively.

31. CHANCE c1900

This image is seen courtesy of Beken of Cowes and shows the tiny Cowes registered ketch *Chance* 13reg./1865 unloading some commodity by wicker basket at Cowes in the old traditional way. Other small traders are about and up ahead a steam tug is getting ready for action at the next jetty. In 1872 the West Cowes registered owner of this little ship was Mrs Jane Cook. By 1900 it was the Rickman family. Some vessels remained with one owner for their entire lengthy careers, others frequently changed hands.

32. PS QUEEN

This twin funnelled paddler came into service in 1902 for Red Funnel initially on the Southampton-Cowes service, but with a speed of 15kts. she could undertake the longer excursions. Earlier paddlers often had their conning positions placed abaft the funnel on the spindliest of bridge platforms. The 345grt *Queen* at least had her bridge forward of the funnels but still no wheelhouse structure at all. This ship carried the name *Mauretania* from 1936 to 1938 for the Cunard White Star Line in order to secure use of that name for their new liner then under construction.

33. Victoria Pier, West Cowes

Believed to date from 1932 this photograph shows two aspects of Cowes maritime activity. One very smart gaff rigged schooner yacht is moored off the pier on the Esplanade. One cargo laden hard working local spritsail barge lies moored beyond and is probably awaiting the tide to go on up to one of the river berths, or Newport. A good number of Medway type spritsail barges became owned in the Solent area – some were actually built at Southampton – as their ability to work in shallow creeks and rivers was just as appreciated here as it was in the Thames Estuary. Typically a sailing barge carried around 130 tons of cargo on a draught of just 6ft. Victoria Pier opened in 1902 principally to give Cowes a slice of the excursion steamer business such as 'round the Island' trips, Beaulieu River, Weymouth, Swanage and Brighton destinations. The pier only extended 170ft out into the fairway and its shortness was also reflected in its lifespan – being demolished in 1961. The concert hall on the end went ten years earlier.

LORD ELGIN
LORD ELGIN

← 34. PS LORD ELGIN

Launched in 1875 the 198grt iron hulled *Lord Elgin* originally performed in the standard passenger excursion work of the day at Bournemouth. In 1908 she passed into the Red Funnel fleet only to be converted two years later for cargo work. Her ornate saloons and passenger facilities were stripped and a large mainmast and derrick installed on the after deck for cargo handling. The fore deck was cleared and bulwarks altered to permit carriage of any wheeled traffic on offer. She then set about making one daily trip cross-Solent from Southampton to Cowes six days per week carrying anything from small packages to herds of livestock. With more modern vessels entering service post WW2 *Lord Elgin* was retired and went for scrap in Southampton in 1955. In the photograph (post WW2), the ship has her later peculiar 'V' fronted wooden wheelhouse and plain design paddle box louvres replacing the original ornate style. Red Funnel also converted the 1885 built paddler *Her Majesty* for car carriage and the 1883 built *Princess Helena* for cars and cargo.

35. The Floating Crane

Southampton's giant floating crane is seen here arriving at Cowes c1930 in the care of one of Alexander Towing's steam tugs at the bow, and probably two of Southern Railway's at the stern. The type of railway stock being transported to Medina Wharf is not too clear to see, although one vehicle end looks more like a Ryde Pier tram replacement. Electric trams were replaced by the Drewry petrol powered versions at about this time, and they would last until the 1969 closure of the Tramway. The fact that Southern Railway owned Southampton Docks and the floating crane must have made such logistical operations simple to plan. St. Helens Quay also saw railway stock movements following the opening of the Bembridge line in 1882.

36. MV MEDINA

This little motor ferry built by Thorneycrofts of Southampton 342grt./1931 marked a significant leap forward from Red Funnel's reliance on paddle steamers. *Medina* could carry a few cars on the after deck and she was powered by twin Gardner diesels and twin screws. She was not a fast ship though, and a change to Crossley engines pushed her speed up from 11 to 13kts. Replaced by a purpose built car ferry in 1962 she went out to Gibraltar for further service before returning to the UK in static clubhouse/restaurant roles such as at Brighton Marina in the 1970s. In the photograph she is carrying a fine selection of 1930s saloon cars all in the customary black livery of the day.

37. MV VECTA →

Despite the appearance of the little *Medina* in 1931, Red Funnel were evidently not totally convinced about the transition to motor power as they ordered another paddler for 1936 delivery. This would be the famous PS *Gracie Fields* which sadly became a WW2 loss en route back from Dunkirk. In 1938 the *Vecta* 630grt. was built and entered service in 1939 on the Southampton-Cowes route. She had the same advanced Voith-Schneider propulsion system seen on the SR's *Lymington*, however following WW2 she was refitted with diesel electric propulsion, standard screws and rudders. This ship had a twelve capacity forward enclosed car deck. She went to the Bristol Channel for further service in 1965 and was scrapped in 1996.

38. MV NORRIS CASTLE (1) →

As we have already seen, Red Funnel tackled the growing motor vehicle cross-Solent trade by converting early paddlers, or furnishing limited space for cars on their newer motor ferries. Following WW2 demand rapidly accelerated for car and commercial vehicle carriage to the IOW on all routes. Red Funnel purchased an ex 1942 built 473grt landing craft in 1947 for conversion to bow and side loading of vehicles. Under the name *Norris Castle* this ship entered service in 1948 and could carry 30 cars. In cargo terms the vessel replaced the ancient *Lord Elgin. Norris Castle* remained in service until 1962 when purpose built tonnage appeared.

39. SS UPTON

A vessel with a somewhat different profile to most of the Solent area ferries, this little steamer had started life as a 'ferry cross the Mersey' in 1925. She was built at Birkenhead for the Mayor, Aldermen and Burgesses of the County Borough of Birkenhead. At 374grt *Upton* appeared on the Solent in 1947 when a shortage of ships prevailed after WW2. She operated on the Southampton-Ryde Pier route for Red Funnel after a period on the Bournemouth to Swanage service. Her local career lasted for just a few years.

40. CARISBROOKE CASTLE

A quantum leap for Red Funnel occurred in 1959 when John I. Thorneycroft of Woolston, Southampton turned out this vessel. Of 620grt; she could carry 42 cars via bow door entry only, a deck turntable being employed to turn the cars around for disembarkation. Later improved variants of this design were: *Cowes*, *Osborne* and a new *Norris Castle(2)*.

41. NETLEY CASTLE

This ship became Red Funnel's first true double ended vehicle ferry upon entry into service in 1974. At 1,183grt, she would be the largest cross-Solent motor ferry of the day and could handle more of the growing number of larger commercial vehicles then appearing on the roads. She became the last vehicle ferry capable of loading cars at West Cowes pontoon in the early 1990s.

43. White's crane and the SS EVANGER →

In looking at trades, cargoes and the ships involved during the last two centuries at least a passing reference to local ship building is essential. Wooden ship building occurred at several locations on the Island over the centuries, such as on the Medina at Cowes and Hurstake (Newport), Wootton Creek and St. Helens. Records for Cowes show an early launching for Queen Elizabeth I in 1588. Island ship building received its biggest boost when Thomas White of Broadstairs, Kent decided that the local beach yard in that town was a bar to the development of his growing business. In 1803 he moved west to Cowes where space and depth of water would permit construction of larger ships, especially for the nearby Navy at Portsmouth.From 1860 onwards the firm became J. Samuel White and over the next 162 years (from 1803), Cowes would turn out wooden, thence steel vessels of many types for the Royal and Merchant Navies as well as foreign orders. Lifeboat building also became a major concern as did periodic repair of ships. In this photograph from c1922 we see the Norwegian steamer *Evanger* 3,869grt./1920 in for voyage repairs, and berthed near to the 1911 built White's hammerhead crane. Whatever malady affected the ship she remained in service for owners Westfal-Larsen of Bergen, and then several Hong Kong owners before scrapping there in 1958. Ship building at Cowes (White's Falcon Yard) ceased in 1965.

42. BALMORAL

Seen here arriving at Cowes in the 1960s on her regular run from Southampton *Balmoral* 688grt./1949 served until 1968. See photograph No.14 for her later history.

44. Cowes Floating Bridge c1900 ↓

The River Medina ensured that Cowes developed as two completely separate towns, East and West. As early as 1740 the right to operate a ferry across the river was granted to the Robertson family. In 1840 provision was made for a horse ferry and in 1859 the first steam powered chain guided ferry went into service for the Cowes Ferry Company. Fares were one penny for passengers later reduced to just a halfpenny and remained as such until the 1950s. Red Funnel bought the business in 1868 and continued to operate it until 1901 when an Act of Parliament saw its control pass to the local council authority. Red Funnel did however operate a foot passenger launch service across the river from 1867 until the outbreak of WW2.

1. The Long 'reign' of the Coal Trade

Coal from the North East of England had been brought South in small merchant sailing ships for centuries before the start of the industrial revolution. Iron hulled ships would follow the wooden ones and steel types not so long thereafter. The sudden railway system development nationally from the 1840s onwards, steamships, factories, industry in general and domestic demand, accelerated the need for increasing volumes of coal and the transportation thereof. From the very early 1800s the use of coal for the process of manufacturing 'town gas' further boosted demand, and one century later even greater pressure built on coal demand and movement, as the infant electricity generation industry appeared on the scene. The Island's requirement for coal mirrored that of the mainland except that naturally every last ton had to be brought in by sea. In the last half of the 20th Century coal use began a steady decline as oil, gas and nuclear power production proliferated. Coal's once near total dominance eroded to leave just a miniscule domestic demand here on the Island today.

The Island's early coal requirements were brought in by smacks, ketches, schooners, brigs and sailing barges which mainly would have been unloaded in the creeks and river estuaries. The River Medina 'thoroughfare' between Cowes and Newport received the lion's share of the trade. Some tonnage was landed straight onto the beaches in the time honoured way, when weather and tidal conditions allowed, direct to horse and cart. This certainly occurred at Ryde Sands, Shanklin, Bonchurch and Ventnor. Minor quays such as at Shalfleet in Newtown Harbour also received coal. With the arrival of the railways from 1862 locally, and ships becoming larger, coal would be unloaded at Yarmouth, the River Medina (various locations), Brading Quay, St.Helens (after reclamation of Brading Harbour), and some continued to be landed at Ryde until the inter war years. Rail distribution of coal around the Island radiated out from Medina Wharf at West Cowes and St. Helens Quay. The latter's railway line closed in 1953. Kingston at East Cowes saw the bulk of latterday coal imports to satisfy the demand at the Island's final gasworks and electricity power station.

Island Gasworks supplied by sea

Firstly, a brief general historical note may be of some help. The World's first proper gas supply system evolved from around 1810 when the London Gas, Light and Coke Company became established to illuminate the Capital and provide domestic service. Its advent accelerated the industrial revolution, and would have far reaching consequences as the technology of gas production could be satisfactorily scaled to work in cities, towns, villages and even large country estates. Remarkably the Island's first gasworks went into production at Newport as early as 1820, a mere ten years after the London inauguration. The following somewhat lengthy notes are intended to give the reader an idea of the extent of the local gas industry here on the Island. The sites are visited in turn starting in the West Wight, the main intention being to examine how so much coal arrived on site for the gas generation to take place. As the old 'town gas' production is now fading from the Nation's memory, a brief technical description will follow. North Sea gas and Middle East LNG imports now sustain the gas mains grid.

The Production of Coal Gas

Coal of a type best suited for gas production is heated to 1,000 deg. C in large retorts where gas is separated, leaving coke. Exhausters force the crude gas through various plant processes in order for it to be freed of impurities. Firstly, a condenser chills the hot gas to release the tar content and some ammonia which is drawn off to a reservoir. Next it passes through a water washer and rises through falling water in a scrubber tower, to be cleaned of ammonia. Trays of iron oxide then further purify the gas by removing foul smelling suphuretted hydrogen. Further processes extract naphthalene and benzol. Together with the tar, coke and spent oxide all of these commodities had value and further industrial use. Coke in particular was supplied in vast quantities for both industrial and domestic use, being the original smokeless fuel.

Coal Types

Gas making coal came principally from mines in Northumberland and Durham, bituminous in nature, these contained some 40% of volatile matter. Some of the Newcastle area mines produced good steam coal – ie 20% volatile matter implying less soot and smoke. These coals were suitable for boiler furnaces. Some South Wales mines produced anthracite coals which yielded the least amount (10%) of volatile material. Lancashire coal fields also offered gas and steam type coals, but were later eclipsed by production from the South Yorkshire mines.

Island Gasworks served by sea

Freshwater (West Wight - Salterns)

The Western Yar almost renders the far West Wight as an island and it would prove problematical for gas main laying operations from the outset. In 1901 the above gasworks was commissioned to supply 'town gas' to Freshwater and Totland both of which were becoming popularised. Coal supplies were brought direct from the North -east by coaster or trans-shipment from the local Solent area. This could be barges from Medina Wharf at Cowes, or Southampton. As early as 1902 a dispute arose whereby the Yarmouth Harbour Authority expected landing dues to be paid to them, despite the coal being destined for the far side of the river. Of course the Gas Company's coal did necessitate the opening of the bridge, and did pass right through the middle of the harbour, en route!

In 1903 the well known mainland firm of Fraser and White were delivering the coal with the ketch *Effort* 25reg./1864 so employed. During WW1 coal supplies were difficult to source and had to be found wherever available. In 1916 some 1,250 tons were required with the steamer *Leading Light* bringing in the cargoes. At some point in 1925 one cargo of about 360 tons came in on a steamer named *Samoa*, and this probably represented a theoretical maximum size load for the trip up to the gasworks. Deliveries, no doubt, were made on the fortnightly high spring tide periods. The local barge *Grebe*, an ex Medway sailing barge based at Cowes, also worked to the Gasworks in 1925. At around this time the major shipping and coal firm of Stephenson, Clarke quoted to supply 1,500 tons in 300 ton lots. By 1927 the tonnage required had risen to 2,500pa. In the 20s and 30s various problems arose with the gas main across the Yar Bridge.

Electricity arrived in the West Wight in 1925. Following the 1949 gas industry nationalisation supply became Island wide by mains and in 1957 Salterns became a gas holding station only.

Yarmouth

The town had its own small gasworks close to the mill on the east bank of the River Yar from 1860. Due to the WW1 coal shortages and extremely high coal prices it ceased operation. From 1860 to 1889 coal arrived by barge, probably to the Mill quay next door. From the latter year it would arrive by rail from Medina Wharf, via Newport. The works operated for a short time after WW1 until mains across the river from Salterns took over.

West Cowes

West Cowes first received gas in 1846 when the Cowes Gas, Light & Coke Company opened for business at what is now known as Arctic Road, where the works fronted onto the River Medina. In 1897 the plant was taken over by the West Cowes Urban District Council. Coal arrived directly by sea to a specially built 'finger' pier jutting out into the deeper water of the Medina. An overhead gantry crane and aerial ropeway system enabled coal discharged to be dropped into the stockyard. A short rail siding off the Newport to Cowes line was used for a while additionally. Production ceased here in 1957 upon the opening of the new Kingston Works on the opposite (east) bank of the river.

East Cowes

This works situated between Clarence Road and the river, opened in 1859 for the East Cowes Gas Company. By 1905 Fraser & White were delivering some 2,000 tpa of coal to the plant's timber jetty/wharf arrangement. Lighters and barges were the main means of coal supply often brought just across the river from Medina Wharf. This works had the honour of supplying Queen Victoria's Osborne House with gas, the estate proving to be a worthy and major customer indeed. Other local users were the Naval College,

Ship Builders, Whites and various other industries. In 1907 coke and tar were being shipped out with the latter going to Boulton & Haywood at Totton for their extensive timber treatment processes. West Cowes gasworks closed in 1954 with mains supplies continuing from Newport and Ryde.

Kingston Gas Works

As previously mentioned, 1949 would see massive rationalisation and centralisation of the gas industry generally. This ultimately saw the closure of all of the smaller local plants. At Kingston, East Cowes where a large electricity generating plant had opened in 1928, an adjacent site was chosen for construction of the new Island Gasworks. This would be served by larger colliers at a wharf facility shared with the British Electricity Authority. The new wharf and craneage were to be operated by the Gas Board personnel yet serve both industries. The new Gasworks facility opened for business in 1955 and by 1957 supplied the entire Island. Despite its modernity Kingston Gasworks was to be short lived as by 1968 a gas pipeline reached the Island from Southampton works. By the 1970s North Sea Gas had percolated to all areas just leaving various local works as holding stations.

Newport

A site at Pan Bridge would see Newport's first gasworks start up c1820 and by 1821 the Newport Gaslight Company had been formed. In 1851 a larger site close to the River Medina at Newport Quay opened to be served directly by barges. Pan Works closed in 1857. Operational difficulties arose in 1877 as the newly arrived railway at Newport attempted to corner the market for coal transportation. The railway line cut right through the access to the quay for the Gasworks coal deliveries. Compromise was reached whereby the Railway Company, having got its own way, loaded the coal trucks at Medina Wharf. After cessation of the day's passenger train services through Newport, they would marshal ten, ten ton trucks at a time to be shunted onto the viaduct overlooking the Gasworks. These would be shovel unloaded down a special chute direct into the Gasworks stockyard. In 1957 Newport gas production ceased upon the opening of the Kingston works.

Ryde

The Gasworks at Ryde began production in 1838 at an inland site not too far from the ultimate location of Ryde St. Johns railway station. Coal would be unloaded from vessels sitting ashore on Ryde Sands by way of traditional horses and carts. From about 1877 it is more likely that deliveries came by rail from the East Wight as Brading Quay had become rail connected (and St. Helens Quay later). Later still Medina Wharf would be the supplier. The Ryde plant closed in 1957 under the ongoing rationalisation scheme.

St. Helens

Brading Harbour District Gas Company opened its plant close to the quay side in 1878. A narrow gauge railway transported coal offloaded from the colliers into the works. The standard gauge railway arrived hereabouts from Brading in 1882. By the 1930s local gas supply in this area came by pipeline from the Ryde works.

Sandown

The Sandown Gas and Coke Company Works opened for business at Avenue Road in 1862. By 1937 the East Wight Gas Company was supplying Sandown, Shanklin and Ventnor. In 1938 Sandown Works closed with supplies now piped from Shanklin.

Shanklin

In 1865 the Shanklin Gaslight Company supplied the area and would itself be coal supplied by the newly arrived railway. A 200ft rail siding beyond the station supplied the gasworks. In 1932 the works amalgamated to form the Shanklin and Ventnor Gas Company. Production ceased in 1957 on completion of Kingston Works.

Ventnor

1866 saw the formation of Ventnor Gas and Water Company with the gas plant situated at the eastern end of the seafront. Despite the exposed nature of the shoreline here, it was served directly by sea from the beach given suitable weather and tide levels for the ships, by traditional horses and carts. At about this time a branch of the well known family of longshoremen, the Wheelers, built a simple but effective 'mini-port' at what has since become known as Wheelers Bay. Various commodities were handled here as well as coal brought in by schooners, brigs and barges. In 1914 some 2,116 tons of coal came to the nearby gasworks by sea. Ventnor works was situated at the end of what is now called Wheelers Bay Road. It closed for business in 1932 on arrival of piped supplies from Shanklin. A gas holding station remained until 1958.

Local gas industry final notes:

In 1955 a cargo of 560 tons of spent oxide was shipped out from the Kingston Works being remains of iron oxide used in the gas production system. Also, during that year rail transportation of coal to the few remaining Island gasworks gave way to road haulage. This left Medina Wharf to serve the coal requirements of the few remaining steam railway engines still at work at that time, plus domestic tonnage. Steam power on the Island's railways ceased operation at the very end of 1966, thereby bringing an era to a close.

Electricity Generation on the Island

General Historical note:

The first electrical supply in England was said to be the illumination of the streets at Godalming in 1881 utilising power generated from the waters of the River Wey. Cables were laid along the roadside gutters as no legislation existed to require their safe burial. Parliament passed the first and vital Electric Lighting Act in 1882 thus remedying such deficiency. In the early years no common standards existed for AC, DC or actual voltage around the Country. In 1927 the Government established the Central Electricity Board to oversee national standardisation of systems. The story of electrical power generation here on the Island began almost a century after the birth of the local gas industry. A brief timetable may be of interest although coal shipments would have been substantial only from 1928 until around four decades ago.

1898 The Ventnor Electric Light and Power Company came into existence.
1899 Renamed Isle of Wight Electric Light and Power Company.
1900 Newport began to be supplied by the Newport Electric Light Company
1903 Most of the Island served by the Isle of Wight Electric Company except West Wight, Yarmouth and Freshwater.
1926 The Company gained authorisation to supply the entire Island.
1928 The first major coal fired power station opened at Kingston, East Cowes.
1931 Finally, Yarmouth Electric Light Company was acquired by the IOW Electric Light and Power Company.
1937 Kingston Power Station variously enlarged by this date.
1948 April saw the Nationalisation of the electricity supply industry under the jurisdiction of the British Electricity Authority (B.E.A.)
1954 Re-branded as the Central Electricity Authority (C.E.A.)
1955 Kingston Power Station again enlarged with the collier berth improved to take ships of up to around 2,000 tons capacity. New craneage on the wharf would be operated by Gas Board personnel to the mutual benefit of both the nationalised industries.
1960 -1980 Installation of a gas pipeline across the Solent would be followed by under sea power connections to the mainland.
2012 Kingston's modern Power Station remains on permanent standby for start-up using gas / oil firing in the event of undersea cable damage or malfunction.

45. SS's ABANA, NELL JESS, ELLINGTON & T.G. HUTTON

A number of the images within this book have appeared before but are of such overall interest as to include again. Four sizeable steamers are moored here together at the original layout Medina Railway Wharf c1900. Close inspection reveals three of the four still carry sails brailed to the masts and the vessel nearest the wharf, *Abana* 729grt./1871, has very old fashioned wooden taffrails around the poop. The *Nell Jess* 496grt./1896 has engines aft, *T.G.Hutton* 703grt./1893 and *Ellington* also 703grt/1882 complete the line up. The wooden finger pier type wharf was built and opened in 1877 by the Cowes and Newport Railway Company to attract the increasing bulk cargoes, especially inbound coal, to the railways.

46. SS CAMBERWAY →

A 782grt./1919 built steam coaster, this vessel seen here in the 1920s at the unaltered original wharf layout, was owned by the Sunderland Steamship Company but managed by Freer & Dix. Following the Railway Grouping of 1923 the Southern set about rebuilding Medina Wharf into a straight quayside arrangement, including installation of new overhead unloading gantries to serve the ships and stockyard. Coal imports regularly totalled around 150,000 tpa. right through until the 1960s when consumption tailed off drastically.

47. SS TIRYDAIL →

The closeup scene dates from the 1930s and shows the new coal facilties provided by the Southern Railway which undoubtedly speeded up handling. The old steamer dates from 1918 and had an interesting history. *Tirydail* 650grt, 900dwt. was built, unusually, near Chepstow in Monmouthshire for Cleeves Western Valleys Anthracite Company Ltd. of Swansea. Sold to F.T. Everard of London in 1926 she would serve them until 1946 before changing hands twice more. The ship was finally lost at sea en route from Garston to Cork in 1952. She still had an open bridge when photographed at Medina Wharf.

CAMBERWAY
SUNDERLAND

48. SS POLGRANGE

This image is seen courtesy of The Isle of Wight Steam Railway archive and more clearly shows the size and scope of the Southern Railways' recently installed overhead gantry crane arrangement at Medina Wharf, c1930. The steamer alongside is identified as the *Polgrange* 804grt./1920 built at Workington. She had previously been named *Ardshean* and then *Edenwood* before registering at Liverpool under the ownership of Brunswick Shipping Company Ltd. Compared to many of her cohort coasters and colliers trading at this time, the ship has a substantially built modern bridge and enclosed wheelhouse. Many were still open with just canvas 'dodgers' for protection. *Polgrange* would not be a lucky ship though, as during one of the notorious North to South coastal convoys around 'hell-fire' corner, she sank following attack in the Dover Strait en route to Portsmouth with coal in July 1940.

↙ 49. SS BONAWE

Just visible across the Medina is a line of coal wagons on the railway sidings approach to Medina Wharf (far right) as seen in the Camberway photograph. The small steam coaster in the foreground is the Scottish owned *Bonawe* 357grt./1919. When photographed in 1929 this vessel also had an old fashioned open bridge and was far from her normal trading areas on the West coast of Scotland. She belonged to J. & A. Gardner of Glasgow who had begun as quarry owners in the late 1800s. By 1900 slate and granite cargoes were being shipped out in steam coasters and the fleet expanded over the next few years. Bonawe was named after the Company's granite quarry on Loch Etive. Gardners' later went over to motor ships and expanded into various other trade areas. The coal trade to South Coast ports often drew in 'strangers' in the 1920s and 30s when cargoes elsewhere were hard to come by. Kingston Wharf at this time with its simple Scotch derrick crane, hopper and hand propelled narrow gauge rail wagons had yet to be upgraded in capacity terms. As already noted, the facility could take colliers of up to 2,000 tons dwt for both the gas and electricity undertakings, post 1955.

50. SS MENDIP

After Nationalisation of the electric power supply industry in 1948 various orders were placed for different size classes of colliers to serve Southern power stations from the North east ports. The smallest size group consisted of some ten vessels to serve West Country installations from Poole Harbour, round to North Somerset. The ships were all of 1,362grt, 1,700dwt, six of which carried '*Poole*' names. *Mendip*, built in 1950, a typical example, could berth at the enlarged Kingston facility post 1955.

51. VECTIS ISLE

The Dutch built coaster *Badzo* came to Vectis Shipping's local fleet in 1959 where she took the name *Vectis Isle* and immediately became their largest vessel. A typical Dutch coaster arrangement, she had a single 'tabernacled' mast and two derricks. These would be later removed in deference to the trend for shore craneage to handle cargoes. The ship had been built in 1939 and measured just 213grt./265dwt. In 1970 she was sold to Panamanian owners for further trading.

52. GAZELLE →

Steel hulled and built in Holland in 1904 this vessel was one of a dozen similar barges with names all ending in 'ic', and belonging to E.J. & W. Goldsmith, of London they were nicknamed 'iron pots'. *Runic* became *Gazelle* in 1951 and already she had been converted to a motor barge, from the original spritsail sailing rig. In the photograph taken at Charlestown, Cornwall in the 1950s it is evident that she still carries one simple sail on the foremast to aid progress with favourable winds. In 1953 a new wheelhouse and more powerful twin engines and screws were fitted. She motored on for Vectis Shipping into the 1970s as did sister barge *Oceanic*.

53. The River Medina with Osborne House beyond, in 1849 →

This image is from another wonderful engraving from the local Brannon family collection, and shows an extremely unspoilt rural Medina valley scene looking from West to East Cowes with ships in the Solent beyond. Almost inevitably one of the many Cowes ketches has been illustrated as she makes her way up stream to Newport four miles away, on the rising tide. The little trader could well have been the *Bee* (see No.55).

GAZELLE

G. Brannon, del. et sc.
DISTANT VIEW OF OSBORNE
FROM THE WEST COWES ROAD, ISLE OF WIGHT.
AND SHOWING MEDINA RIVER WHIPPINGHAM CHURCH & EAST COWES PARK

54. CLENWOOD

Dating from May 1928 this photograph taken on the Medina mud upriver from East Cowes shows the Associated Portland Cement Manufacturers barge *Clenwood* 81grt./1911. Rochester built, she was a typical Medway sailing barge and probably loaded about 130 tons of cargo. At about the time of the photograph, and like many of her kind, she had become motorised. She is seen here in temporary lay-up with sails ready to deploy and a lightweight access gangway has been rigged to the shore over the mud. The shallow nature of these craft is plain to see and jokingly it was often said that they could 'float on the dew, or on wet grass'.

55. BEE

An image that has appeared many times over the years – the little Cowes ketch *Bee* built at East Cowes by Hansen in 1801 had a truly astonishing lifespan. She traded for Shepard Bothers of Newport for 116 years. Unlike most of her cohort barges this one has a round stern and would never be motorised. Even after retiring from trade she was not cut up but filled with concrete as part of a jetty foundation. The photograph probably dates from the ship's later years as visible on the sail are the letters 'Established 1800' – a reflection of her owners' company longevity. The name *Bee* has appeared more than once locally, the last being a Faversham built motor barge from 1927.

56. DEBOURNE

Another steel hulled Dutch built vessel, the motor coaster *Debourne* 104grt./1925 is seen here in some predicament, evidently where she should not have been. This vessel joined the Island Transport Company's fleet in 1936, remaining until 1953. Island Transport had been formed as a subsidiary of J. Samuel White & Co. Ltd, to convey their own cargoes and others across the Solent. Their 91ft motor barge *Calbourne* survives to this day at Newport.

57. MURIUS

Caught on camera here in Essex at Maldon, sitting in a floating dock is the ex Vectis Shipping, and later, Williams Shipping motor barge *Murius* 125grt./1962. She was one of the last motor cargo barges built for cross-Solent trade. The photograph dates from 2008.

58. The Royal Yacht BRITANNIA

With the Queen's diamond jubilee celebrations this year it seems appropriate to remind ourselves that this splendid vessel attended many Cowes week regattas over the years between 1954 and the early 1990s. Built by the famous John Brown yard on Clydebank, *Britannia* displaced 4,700 tons and had steam turbine twin screw propulsion, capable of reaching some 21kts. The ship served the Monarch and the Nation until 1997 when withdrawn from service and taken to Leith Docks, Edinburgh where she remains in fine fettle, afloat and open to the public.

59. THV PATRICIA →

This Trinity House buoy tender on occasion undertook Royal Yacht duties following the withdrawal of *Britannia* and indeed had fine accommodation for a few passengers seeking an unusual type of trip. She is seen here moored off East Cowes in June 2001. The 2,639grt vessel was built in 1982.

60. TARWAY →

This is an unremarkable little motor barge indeed, but one that has had three widely differing careers. Built in 1955, the 80grt./110dwt *Tarway* originally lived up to her name as she collected that commodity from gasworks in the Solent area for further processing. Newport Quay was just one such loading point. Later the ship moved west to Teignmouth in Devon where she was fitted with a sand suction pump and pipe to supply the local building trade. In 2003 *Tarway* returned to the River Medina to work in the aggregate trade from Southampton. In the photograph taken in 2003 the dredging apparatus is still carried but was later removed.

61. RED JET 4

Seen arriving at West Cowes in 2003 is the newly acquired *Red Jet 4*. Red Funnel's earlier conventional passenger vessels already described within, had long been replaced by various hydrofoil and fast catamaran types. The Italian built '*Shearwater*' class arrived from 1969 and worked the Southampton route until the appearance of the Red Jet cats in the early 1990s. *Red Jet 4*, capable of up to 34kts has water jet propulsion. In the background Crescent Shipping's tanker *Barmouth* is taking on the pilot for the run in to Kingston Oil Depot.

62. RED EAGLE →

By the late 1980s both Red Funnel and Wightlink had to consider enlarging their vehicle carrying capacity due to increasing demand, especially from the number of large articulated trucks now required to make Island deliveries. Also, at this time all general cargo to and from the Island had forsaken the traditional barges for the roll-on, roll-off method. Door to door goods transportation, thereby eliminating double handling, ensured the barges lost their ability to compete economically, except for a few bulk commodities in transit. For Red Funnel, the first of three large 'Raptor' class ferries appeared in 1993 *Red Falcon* 2,881grt; *Red Osprey* followed and the last, *Red Eagle* arrived in 1996. Still traffic volumes grew so in the early 2000s all three ships were sent away in turn to be enlarged (jumboised) in order to cope for the future. In this photograph *Red Eagle*, the one with the higher bridge, is seen in her 'as built' form in 2000.

63. BERGEN CASTLE →

During the absence of each Raptor class vessel for enlargement, this curious looking ex Norwegian car ferry seen arriving at East Cowes in 2003, temporarily helped maintain schedules. Over on the West Cowes side can be seen the excursion vessel *Wight Scene* and a smart white hulled two masted schooner yacht.

RED FUNNEL

64. RED FALCON

Seen in 2004 the much altered ship now sports rebuilt accommodation with an all new through upper car deck, accessible to the shore at each end by raised links. The main deck would thus be freer for the stowage of commercial vehicles, etc. In practical terms Red Funnel solved their capacity problem brilliantly, and did not need new ships. Perhaps though, aesthetically the modifications are a bit stark in profile compared to the original neat design layout.

65. WIGHT SCENE →

Seen departing her home base of West Cowes in July 2010 *Wight Scene* is setting off for Portsmouth Harbour and a day's sightseeing thereabouts for the tourists. She is operated by Solent and Wightline Cruises.

66. OCEAN SCENE →

Blue Funnel Cruises today provide local excursions and one or two regular trips about the Southampton/ Cowes / Portsmouth areas. In this September 2010 photograph the vessel is helping out with the crowds involved in the Island's second big pop festival of the year, 'The Bestival'. The Southampton based ship is of a catamaran type now quite often found around the country carrying out leisurely trips in rivers and sheltered waters. These craft are really the true modern successors to the excursion paddle steamers of old.

WIGHT SCENE

OCEAN SCENE

67. Royal Yacht Squadron works in 2005

In November a large floating crane has been brought over from Southampton and is engaged in lowering pre-fabricated concrete breakwater sections to form a new mini-harbour in front of the Royal Yacht Squadron. The tug *Chiefton* has brought the barge laden with the sections to the West Cowes site.

68. ARCO DEE →

This motor dredger 1,309grt./1990 has just deposited a load of sea dredged aggregate ashore at Cowes, and is heading back to sea for the next cargo. The end of the new breakwater described above is visible to the left whilst the outer end of the new Jubilee Landing Stage for visiting craft lies to the right. The photograph dates from October 2011.

69. BELEM →

The beautifully restored barque *Belem* is seen here alongside the Jubilee Pontoon in September 2010. The French-built and flagged ship had once spent much time in Cowes. Her story started in 1896 with construction at Nantes as a deep sea sailing merchant ship to be engaged in trade to South America and the Caribbean Sea for her French owners. In 1914 the Duke of Westminster bought her for conversion to luxury yacht status. Later, in 1921 the Hon. Arthur Ernest Guiness bought the ship and had her renamed *Fantome II*. He died in 1949 but under both British owners the ship frequented Cowes events. In a 1930s Mercantile List the ship is said to be of 436reg.tons and 562grt, registered in Southampton and powered by a 480hp motor at that time. In due course the ship found her way back to French owners for restoration as *Belem* by the Belem Foundation. As *Fantome II* she had remained in Cowes from 1939 until 1947. The little yellow hulled ketch in the foreground is the *Black Rose* of Maldon.

70. IRENE

Another old timer and ex trading vessel seen at Cowes in May 2011 is the ex West Country ketch *Irene* 67reg./1907 built at Bridgwater, Somerset where she was the last such built. For decades she traded from there for owners Colthurst, Symons in the Bristol Channel and Irish Sea areas. Later she became a private yacht moored on the Thames but even later travelled far afield. Seriously damaged by fire a few years ago she has now been painstakingly rebuilt. When seen at Cowes she was on a 'token' cargo run from Bordeaux to London with a promotional shipment of the Nouveau Beaujolais.

71. RED JET 5 →

Berthing at West Cowes pontoon in June 2010 is the latest addition to the Red Funnel Hi-speed fleet. *Red Jet 3* has just vacated the berth.

72. OCEAN CAT →

A far cry from the comfortable local catamaran ferries, the heavily constructed workboat catamaran *Ocean Cat* is entering Cowes in September 2010. Designed and equipped for rigorous offshore survey or maintenance work, there are few frills about this tough workhorse of a craft. She is evidently geared up for nudging up to offshore structures by way of the massive fixed tyre bow fenders. An hydraulic crane is fitted on the foredeck.

RedJet
Turn up and take off
www.redfunnel.co.uk
RED JET 5
SOUTHAMPTON

OCEANCAT

73. TENACIOUS

Launched in 2000 at Southampton, this sail training vessel carries a barque rig – two of the three masts being square rigged. Passing beyond the excursion catamaran *Solent Cat* heads home to Cowes in 2010.

74. ALICE →

In fine fettle seen here motoring out of the Medina in June 2010 is the Medway sailing barge *Alice* 50reg./1895, built at Maidstone, Kent. As already described herein, such barges were once common in the Solent area as the shallower creeks were not unlike those of their Thames and Medway counterparts. *Alice* is often to be seen moored at Portsmouth's Gunwharf development beneath the Spinnaker Tower. A modern motor cruiser was determined to get into the photograph and has rather spoilt the graceful stern profile of the old barge. Today, a number of 'retired' barges work in the hospitality trade in the Thames, Medway, Essex, Kent and Solent areas.

75. MT HUMBER ENERGY →

A great variety of coastal tankers and tank barges have kept the Island supplied with fuel over the last century since the internal combustion engine first appeared. Oil, petrol and diesel engines successively proliferated in that order from around the time of WW1. A local supplier in 2010 was the ex Humber tank barge *Humber Energy* 380grt/ 650dwt, built in 1983. In this photograph she is just entering Cowes and is displaying her owner's name on the tank top side, John H. Whitaker Ltd; and flying their large houseflag additionally.

HUMBER ENERGY

76. GOOLE STAR

Another ex Humber trader this time in the form of the dry cargo barge *Goole Star* 210grt./1970 is now working in the aggregate trade to the Medina and Solent areas. Seen entering the river in this 2009 image she is probably heading 'home' to Newport. The old Princess flying boat construction hanger still sports the largest Union flag in the world, and can be seen over at East Cowes beyond the barge.

77. GRETA C →

This photograph and the following two are shown courtesy of Fotoflite. In 1969 the barge and small coaster operating firm of Vectis Shipping became the fledgling Carisbrooke Shipping Company. This firm soon began acquiring good quality second hand tonnage for the coastal and near Continental trades. In this image *Greta C.* 698grt./1,154dwt/ of 1966 has joined the fleet. Originally built for Everards as their *Actuality* she carried a set of four derricks to work cargo. The central mast and cargo gear was later removed and reliance placed on shore cranes. The ship sailed on for Carisbrooke Shipping until 1988.

78. MARK C →

Unit sizes were on the increase in 1986 when another ex Everard motor ship was acquired in the form of the ex *Security 1*,596grt./ 2,778dwt and dating from 1971. This ship had been launched without cargo gear as that trend grew.

79. JANET C

By the mid 1990s Carisbrooke were operating some fifteen ships within the 2,000 to 4,500 ton ranges. In 1998 *Janet C.* 2,748grt./4,290dwt – a new-building, joined the fleet representing a new class and standard type of bulker. A fleet totalling some twenty ships were in service by 2002. This progressive and very successful Company has since more than doubled in size, entered a number of international areas of trade and operates cargo vessels in the 5,000 to 19,000 ton range, some suitable for container carriage and others crane fitted. An amazing growth story indeed.

80. MTB BLADE RUNNER ONE →

In June 2010 two '*Blade Runner*' barges were carrying various loads across the Solent since mainstream production of the Vestas wind turbine blades at Newport had ceased. In the photograph cargo consisted of a new ocean racing yacht hull, two containers and sundry items. By virtue of their specialist trade the barges had to be very long, relatively narrow, and shallow in construction, able to proceed in either direction in tight spaces without turning around if required.

81. SAN MARINI →

One of the 'L.A.D.' (low air draught) type coasters becoming popular for river/sea trading in the 1970s, this little ship had four previous names. When seen entering Cowes in 2010, she had become registered at the Georgian Black Sea port of Batumi. The Georgian flag can be seen proudly flying from the stern. Whatever the ship's prospects at the time she would go for scrap one year later. *San Marini* 1,300grt/1977.

BMW ORACLE Racing
MTB BLADE RUNNER ONE

SAN MARINI

82. BRITANNIA (a new yacht), and CARDIGAN BAY

The Solent based ex U.S.Army floating crane has been brought over to East Cowes to lift the massive hull of the new-building *Britannia* out of the water onto the concrete apron for fitting out to commence. The hull had arrived from Archangel, Northern Russia where construction had been carried out over several years. The project involves building a complete replica of King George V's private racing yacht of the same name. The original vessel 115reg./1893 had been stripped of all fittings and sunk off the South coast of the Island in accordance with the King's wishes, in 1936. (See No.182). One of local boat builder South Boats' new offshore wind farm support boats *Cardigan Bay* is also fitting out nearby in this March 2012 photograph.

83. SWAN DIANA →

Seen passing inwards by the Cowes floating bridge terminal in 2007 is the rather basically designed *Swan Diana* 2,113grt./1983 one of a group of similar ships. This one has been fitted with self discharging gear. This includes a conveyor and unloading arm etc. Today Naval architects produce some ultra efficient vessels but many lack the graceful lines and design of earlier merchantmen. The ship was on her sixth name when seen here working the aggregate trade.

84. SWANLAND →

In 2010 the *Swanland* 1,978grt./1977 was captured at the same spot heading to Kingston Wharf, East Cowes with an aggregate cargo. Of Dutch origin, this ship also had been a recent convert to self discharging operations. Sadly, with some loss of life she sank in heavy weather whilst carrying out a similar voyage, this time from Llandulas, North Wales to Cowes, in November 2011 with a cargo of limestone.

SWAN DIANA

SWANLAND

85. BEAUMONT

Seen departing Cowes in March 2012 is the pride and flagship of Faversham Ships, the *Beaumont* 2,545grt./3,820dwt./2005. This smart liveried, well kept vessel has just sailed from Medina Wharf and well illustrates how the size of visiting cargo ships has grown over the last few decades. In railway and nationalised industries ownership, Medina and Kingston Wharves were rarely visited by ships of greater than 2,000 tons capacity. Today Faversham Ships operate a modern fleet of ten vessels.

86. Cowes Chain Ferry in 2011 →

Ending another of its interminable Medina crossings from West Cowes, the present ferry is just about to 'touch down' at East Cowes under the care of the operator in his little control box above. Now around thirty five years old, consideration is being given to a replacement craft for this vital link. There has also been some possible good news for the preservation of Samuel White's 1911 built hammerhead crane. This centenarian is now in dire need of some renovation, and is on English Heritage's 'structures at risk' list. When serving the shipyard the crane was rated at 80 tons lifting capacity but this reduced some years ago to just a few tons. The tug moored beneath bears the unusual name of *Sir Silas*.

87. TOP-UP →

It would not be easy to find a bunker tanker smaller than this one. The locally based *Top-up* is seen here in 2006 heading downstream past East Cowes yacht marina.

BEWARE
OF
CHAINS
7.5
TONS

88. BARDSEY at Kingston Wharf

Today the wharf area once shared by gas and electricity undertakings now performs two very different functions with reception of the Island's fuel requirements, and cargoes of ballast and aggregates. In this 2001 photograph Crescent Shippings' coastal tanker *Bardsey* 1,144grt./1981 has barely started pumping her cargo ashore. One of Kingston Power Station's twin chimneys is visible far right.

89. RIX MERLIN

With the power station chimney towering above Rix Shippings' little motor tanker 496grt./750dwt./2005 is unloading her regular cargo to the oil depot at Kingston in this 2010 photograph. Built on the Humber this smart little ship is sadly almost unique for recent times, when virtually every merchant vessel of any size starts life in far Eastern shipyards.

90. RIX MERLIN, at sea

Very small coastal tankers are something of a rarity today around the European shores as refineries and storage depots employ larger and larger vessels in order to keep costs down. Only where islands present special cases can one find employment for tiny tankers. The old established firm of J.R. Rix of Hull turned from cargo vessel operation to coastal tanker work and bunkering some years ago. From their Humberside base area they now operate further afield and have even converted a number of redundant small cargo ships into useful little tankers. In this aerial photograph courtesy of Fotoflite, the *Rix Merlin* looks to be a suitably tough little ship for the trade. She is fitted with an hydraulic long arm hose handling crane and modern regulations have insisted that mast hoops be fitted for crew safety aloft.

91. WINDSTAR

Beyond the inevitable forest of yacht masts at East Cowes Marina lies Medina Wharf on the opposite West Cowes side of the river. Following cessation of coal imports after the railway days, the wharf developed as a multi-purpose facility for the import or export of any bulk commodity. The main cargoes handled are grain outward, ballast and other aggregates, and timber cargoes inward. In this 2010 photograph the Swedish operated *Windstar* 2,237grt./1991 has all but finished unloading a cargo of packaged timber from the Baltic.

2. The Timber Trade

Towards the end of the timber ship building period, no doubt most of the usable Island material had gone. As ship construction went over to iron then steel hulls, generally the problem would at least in part be resolved. However the building trade had to keep pace with the Island's housing and other industrial timber requirements, so imports increased. Morey's started importing sawn Baltic timber in 1873 and some three or four shiploads were required per annum. Arriving in vessels too large to proceed up-river to Newport, these cargoes would be unloaded at Medham anchorage, where deeper water moorings could be utilised. The timber was then transported aboard local barges up to Newport Quay and the timber storage sheds. Baltic softwood, sawmill cut into various sizes, was stowed by hand on the cargo ships traditionally in the loading ports, until a few decades ago when metricated packaged timber became the norm for the trade. These packages fitted perfectly into the box shaped holds of modern cargo ships and could be positioned by crane. Discharged similarly, man handling of the timber would no longer be required at all.

92. PS MEDWAY QUEEN

The Dunkirk veteran paddler had retired from her Medway-North Kent-Southend trips in 1963. In September 1965 she arrived in the River Medina after a tow from Kent by way of the Watkins tug *Dhulia*, to be moored at the site of the East Medina Mills at Binfield. Built in 1924 at Troon, Scotland, the 316grt vessel originally had coal fired boilers, later switching to oil firing in 1938. With a team of single minded preservationists working away in the background and after some twenty years on the Island, the ship retuned to Kent on a flat topped barge in 1984. Restoration has proceeded as fast as funds would permit, and after many trials and tribulations along the way it was decided to build a brand new hull. The original had however yielded a 'set of many parts' for ultimate re-installation. A new funnel and paddle boxes were made up some years ago and have sat on the Chatham Dockyard wall overlooking the Medway, awaiting their time for fitting. In due course a revitalised *Medway Queen* should begin a second career.

Map No. 5 Newport →

(1) Blackhouse Quay
(2) Little London, the first electricity generation site
(3) Gasworks site
(4) Coppins Bridge
(5) Chalk pit for rail supply to West Medina Cement Mill.

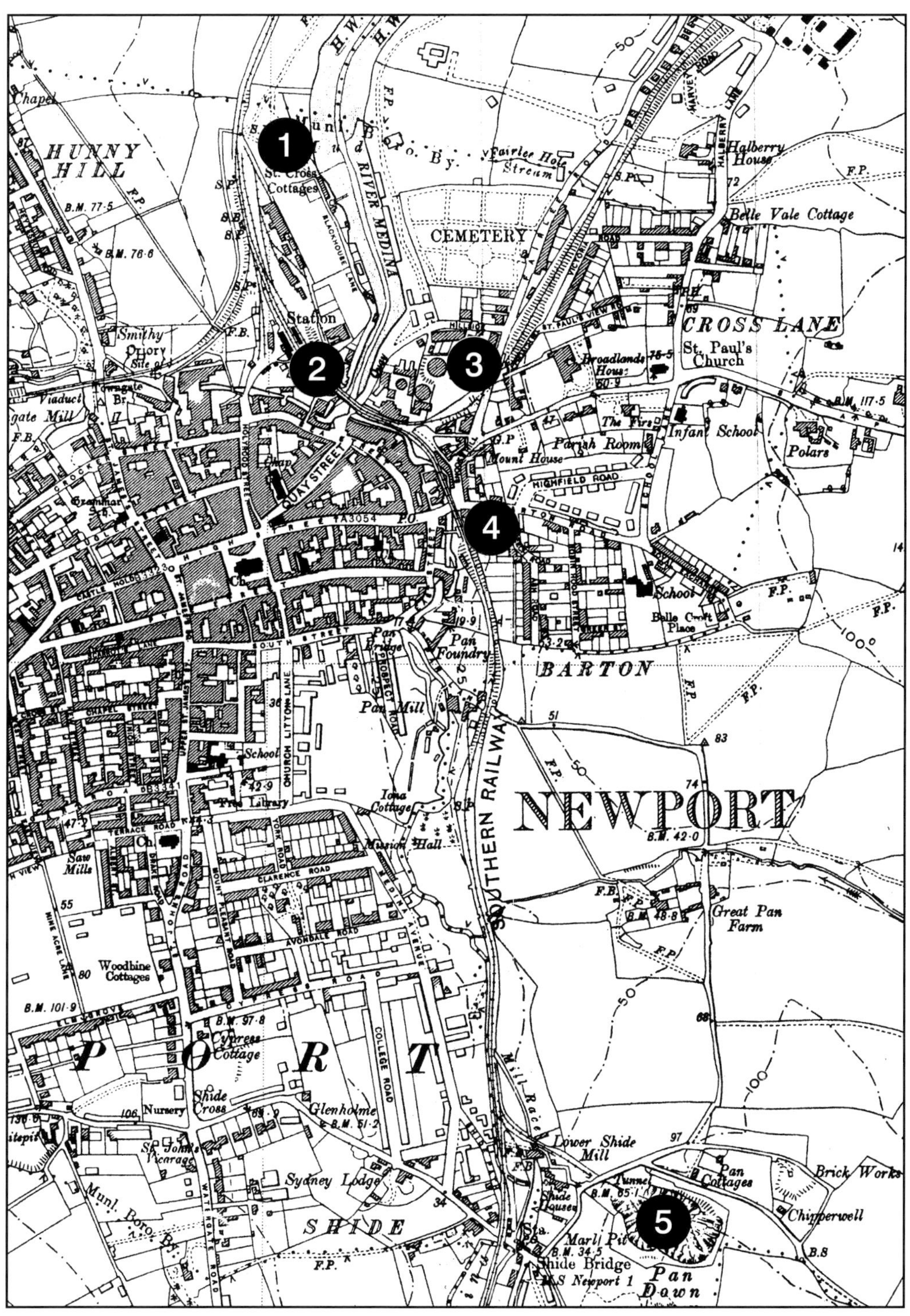

1
2
3
4
5
Chapel
HUNNY HILL
B.M. 77·5
B.M. 76·6
Smithy
Priory Site of
Viaduct
Towngate Br.
gate Mill
F.B.
St. Cross Cottages
Station
RIVER MEDINA
Fairlee Hole Stream
CEMETERY
Halberry House
Belle Vale Cottage
CROSS LANE
St. Paul's Church
Broadlands House
The Firs
Infant School
Polars
Parish Room
Mount House
HIGHFIELD ROAD
QUAY STREET
A3054
P.O.
Grammar Sch.
SOUTH STREET
Pan Bridge
Pan Foundry
BARTON
Belle Croft Place
School
Pan Mill
Free Library
Iona Cottage
Mission Hall
SOUTHERN RAILWAY
NEWPORT
B.M. 42·0
Great Pan Farm
Saw Mills
CLARENCE ROAD
AVONDALE ROAD
Woodbine Cottages
COLLEGE ROAD
P O R T
Cypress Cottage
Nursery
Shide Cross
Glenholme
St. John's Vicarage
Sydney Lodge
SHIDE
Mill Race
Lower Shide Mill
Shide Houses
Tunnel
Pan Cottages
Brick Works
Chipperwell
Marl Pit
Shide Bridge
Pan Down
Munl. Boro. By.

93. PS RYDE

Dating from 1937 the Portsmouth-Ryde paddle ferry 566grt, completed her final Solent excursions in 1969 and then found her way to Binfield for static employment as a night club. Sadly, as *Ryde Queen*, fate was not so kind to this ship with a fire and ultimate dereliction ensuing. The photograph dates from 1995 and shows the old steamer at least still looking relatively intact. The intervening years have not been kind and today minus masts, funnel and most other things, she is steadily collapsing into the Medina mud berth that she has occupied for so long.

94. PS MONARCH

Sitting quietly in the Island Harbour close to the remains of the Ryde and not long after her Island arrival from Kent in 2008, is the delightful little privately built and owned PS *Monarch*. At just 42ft in length she captures beautifully the grace and lines of Victorian paddlers although built in the last couple of decades her engine was said to be one hundred years old! Whilst based on the Island the little ship undertook various special event duties but regular service was not too successful, possibly due to her limitation for twelve passengers, and the nature of the tidal Medina not helping. She left, again by road, for pastures new after a couple of years on the Medina, and later could be seen on the upper reaches of the River Tamar such as at Morwellham Quay Industrial Museum. In the photograph although looking isolated, the paddler is actually in the middle of the yacht basin site that once provided the headwaters for East Medina corn mill workings.

3. Corn Mills and the Grain Trade

At one time some thirty eight watermills and seven windmills were at work grinding corn on the Island for both local consumption and export. The larger tide mills such as at East and West Medina, Wootton Bridge and St. Helens, did a brisk trade directly by sea to the mainland, to the Royal Navy and merchant sailing ships. In 1303 corn was being supplied for Edward I's army fighting in Scotland. 1560 saw the repeal of an oppressive tax law allowing grain to again be shipped away. The term 'corn' implied oats, wheat, barley, maize, peas and beans. By the 1790s the Island was reportedly the 'granary of the Western Counties' and the chief source of malt, salt, flour and biscuit for the Navy. This continued through the 1800s with exports also to London and other Channel ports. The large mills at East and West Medina, near Newport were supplying convict ships from around 1790 as these vessels anchored off Cowes to take final provisions for their long sea voyages ahead. By the 1890s cheap bulk grain imports from North America were severely affecting local grain production. Today with modern strains of cereal crops, grain is again an important Island export with cargoes of up to 3,000 tons departing Medina Wharf on occasions.

95. West Medina Cement Mills

This and several images to follow all relate to the curious changeover phenomena seen at the site as early as 1840. The first image shows in artistic colour style, how the Cement Works would have appeared before 1900, with a variety of commercial trading vessels scattered about the locality.

4. Cement Manufacturing

Around 1840 West Medina corn mill switched to cement manufacturing and would make variations on 'Roman Cement'. Raw materials were brought initially from the mainland by ship or barge but suitable clay could be dug on site for the process. After the railways' local arrival the necessary chalk required could come the three miles by rail from Shide Quarry, South of Newport after 1880. The plant became extensive, but would ultimately close to manufacturing in 1944 when Associated Portland Cement Manufacturers built a larger more modern works at Shoreham. In 1900 this firm had absorbed some twenty six individual cement makers around the country. Cement would then be imported from the Sussex ports and North Kent works by coasters, and later road transport by the vehicle ferries, etc. That changeover occurred in 1987.

96. FERROCRETE

A.P.C.M's own little Faversham built motor coaster *Ferrocrete* 158grt./1927 is seen here in this 1950s photograph courtesy of Fotoflite, at sea and looking very tidy. She carried bagged cement to the Island's West Medina Depot on many occasions and at just 100ft in length could load at Asham Cement Works between Newhaven and Lewes on the Sussex River Ouse. That works closed in 1967 and then supplies came from Shoreham, or North Kent's Greenhithe facility.

97. Cement Mills shipping c1900

The extent of the works is quite apparent in this surprisingly sharp image with much shipping 'on show' alongside the wharves and river bank. There are no less than three steam coasters present, all of which carry some sail, plus one steam barge with a load of chalk. Additionally there are three trading ketches and a couple of river lighters to complete this fascinating industrial scene. It is of course highly likely that periods of intense shipping activity would coincide with the fortnightly spring tides. The larger vessels seen here would certainly have loaded to 10ft to 12ft draught, and required about 15ft of water in the river for safe navigation to sea.

98. The Cement importing facility ↓

This 1983 photograph shows two very different little motor coasters alongside the West Medina Cement Depot wharf. The ex Dutch coaster *Ash Lake* 198grt./1939 has evidently unloaded her cargo and is ready to depart. She was locally owned by Capt. Alf Sheaf. Astern lies one of F.T. Everards' standard XL-400 series motor coasters *Formality* 200grt./400dwt./1968. This ship and one or two sister vessels were fitted out to carry bulk cement cargoes with loading and unloading by shore equipment. Even this more economic form of cement transport would be superceded in just a few years with through deliveries by road trailers from North Kent and the vehicle ferries. On the wharf the bulk cement silo is visible and far right a small oil tank farm has appeared.

99. MT BATSMAN

Just arriving in this 1985 photograph with supplies for the oil depot just mentioned, is Bowker & King's esturial type tanker *Batsman* 215grt./1963. Suitable for 'under the bridges of London' work, the crew will not be bothered with lowering masts, the derrick or radar scanner on this trip. The wharf is evidently also receiving aggregates.

100. A 'new beginning' →

After site clearance another modern industrial function appeared at the old West Medina Mills site – a major research and development facility for Vestas wind turbine blade technology. In 2010 the old wharf was part re-piled for seaborne access. This plant is about one mile further downstream from the original blade building factory at St.Cross, Newport. The 2012 photograph is not the best due to the foreshore being totally in shade, but beyond on the west side a large mobile crane is positioned ready to load extra long blades onto the *Blade Runner Two* barge. One blade is already on the barge's deck.

101. MTB BLADE RUNNER ONE - loading →

This image dates from 2003 and shows the barge's original livery. She is moored at St.Cross with a straddle carrier loading a blade as she sits in the purpose built berth. The narrow nature of the River Medina and its shallow depth rendered it necessary for the two specialist barges to be able to proceed in either direction for short distances without turning around.

102. 'Ship & Launch' pub (c1905)

A happy group of Edwardian children of assorted ages interrupt play to pose for the camera on the west bank of the river. Beyond once stood Hurstake Shipyard which had in earlier years been quite a prolific ship building establishment during the 1700s. The yard survived until about 1830 when as ships grew in size, building moved down river to Cowes. The house by the shipyard became a public house c1839 for local workers. In the photograph Newport Rowing Club had yet to put a second storey onto their boathouse. Oyster fisheries were once of some consequence between here and Cowes and there appears to have been contentious issues over their working.

103. DCI PERELLE →

Blackhouse Quay seen here in 1973 has long been a receiving point for sand and ballast deliveries. In recent years, following the total demise of the general cargo barge traffic on the Medina, the berth has become Newport Harbour's last true commercial wharf, as yachting and associated activities have filled the void. The dredger *DCI Perelle* once served as a landing craft, judging by the almost full width bow door arrangement visible.

104. Blackhouse Quay in 2009 →

A smart looking *Goole Star* has discharged her cargo and awaits the next move. The large red crane is a shore based item beyond. The area above and beyond the quay is now very industrialised and the trees and fields behind the old 'Noah's Ark' have long since vanished. *Goole Star's* previous occupation had been seaweed collection for fertiliser use in the Falmouth / Truro area.

105. 'Noah's Ark' (1906)

An old unwanted barge hull became an unlikely 'Noah's Ark' around 1850, a short distance from Newport Quay on the west bank of the river. It belonged to the Cooper family whose business involved rowing boat hire on the river. The hull steadily grew vertically into an odd boat-shaped clapper boarded cottage. Following Mr Cooper's demise c1900 it was reported that the old hull failed to rise with the tide. Demolition followed and the site adjacent became Shepard Brothers' Model Store (warehouse).

106. SS SPRAY and the Model Store

Spray and sister vessel *Foam* 64grt were both built by Whites' at Cowes in 1897 for Shepard Brothers' cross-Solent trade. Steel hulled and with engines rated at no less than 18hp, they were of course far more efficient than the wind reliant sailing barges. Some attempt could be made to operate to proper sailing schedules although the tidal nature of the Medina did not help much. Relatively few steam barges traded in the Solent area as from WW1 early motor power prospered requiring no stoker or large space lost to coal bunkers. The motor barges ran together with some still active sailing types almost up until WW2. Nevertheless, *Spray* and *Foam* had long useful careers, ending in the towage, salvage and dredging business. In the early 1900s photograph *Spray* is moored right outside her owners' Model Store.

107. ARROW and WELLINGTON

This scene is of great fascination to anyone interested in coastal sailing ship history. The image is dateable to within quite a short period. Shepard Brothers' ketch *Arrow* was built in 1875 and their Model Store appeared in the late 1890s. A smart unidentified topsail schooner lies stern on to the camera close to *Arrow* 20 reg.tons. She survived until 1938. The most interesting vessel is the old *Wellington* 36 reg.tons and built in 1815. She is a typical old time sailing coaster of solid construction and little different to vessels of one hundred years earlier. Bluff bowed, speed in those far off days was not a factor for consideration at all. The ship was owned in 1872 by Thomas Holbrook of Newtown. Later, hulls would become more streamlined with finer bows and overall lighter construction. The eastern shore at Newport had yet to see development as countryside abuts the riverbank. The image is seen courtesy of Carisbrooke Castle Museum.

108. WHIP and a large boiler

Timewise this image is a little out of sequence but not geographically. The rather faded scene is doubly of interest as the wooden hulled motor barge *Whip* 64grt./1922 had been built almost opposite this location. She was launched from the slipway of the delightfully named Odessa Shipyard, for local owner Crouchers Ltd, and powered by a 60hp motor could carry about 100 tons of cargo. The Odessa Yard had been run by the Bishop family since 1883. The cargo onboard consists of an enormous boiler on deck with probably some bulk commodity below in the hold to give stability for the crossing from the mainland. Such large item movement involved much human effort and long lost skills as today, low loader road transport, powerful cranes and technology in general, have simplified such operations. Careful choice of quayside, tidal levels, baulks of timber, horses and human effort would all be required to literally 'roll' the boiler ashore. In 1895 one 16 ton boiler reportedly needed some 22 horses to pull its low trailer through the streets of Newport to the final destination. Of course there was at the time no traffic to cause general gridlock about the place!

109. CHAMOIS →

In this immediate post WW2 scene the quay looks remarkably bare of barge cargoes. *Chamois* 44 reg. tons/1917 and built at Plymouth, was a near sister vessel to No.110. This barge was one of the half dozen or so local craft that bravely made the passage to the Dunkirk beaches for the mass evacuation of soldiers during WW2, in 1940. *MFH, Murius (1), Hound* and *Bat* being similarly deployed while *Bee* (motor version) had to return to England with a wire fouled propeller. In the photograph *Chamois* carries her owner's name Crouchers Ltd, in small lettering near the stern.

110. TALLY-HO →

Wooden hulled and built at Stonehouse, Plymouth in 1912 as a ketch rigged barge, this vessel joined Crouchers' local fleet in 1931. Also of 44grt, she had been motorised with a 60hp engine and, as seen in this photograph, acquired a simple wheelhouse of a design typical of many local barges. This no doubt, would have been very welcome protection for the crew. The mizzen mast became a thing of the past. Owners' names were becoming more prominent and 'Crouchers Ltd' was painted on the after end. Various

sheds and warehouses have appeared beyond. The ship became one of the amalgamated fleet of Pickfords in 1936 totalling some twenty one assorted vessels. In 1948 ownership passed under Nationalisation to the British Transport Commission, thence by 1956 to British Road Services, which dates this image. Other barges in the photograph are *SBL 6* and *MFH,* beyond which lies the Green Store and the brick built Jubilee Stores. The latter now houses offices whilst a car park replaced the Green Store which from 1920 Crouchers Ltd had used as an important distribution warehouse.

111. NEEDLES by the Green Store

The 'day boat' motor barges were still being built for the conventional break-bulk or general cargo cross-Solent services well into the 1960s largely to replace ageing units less able to carry the larger modern loads. *Needles* 93grt./1960 would not achieve a lengthy local trading career, as freight shortly passed to the roll-on, roll-off car ferry system spreading throughout the UK and Europe. Of course the elimination of loading and unloading goods both on the mainland and the Island for the short sea crossing made for much greater efficiency of operation. Stevedores were suddenly redundant as goods could pass from factory to final recipient without unloading the trucks. This 1969 image shows *Needles* moored by the Green Store with another barge just visible on the other side of the river at Odessa Shipyard's slipway. That is the stern of the *Field*, whilst Blackhouse Quay lies beyond. The *Needles* later went to work at a West Coast of Ireland fish farm during the 1980s and was reportedly still there in 2000.

112. The 'Pirate Ship' - NORA-AV-VEN

Berthed alongside the Green Store in this 1991 scene, the public attraction known as the 'Pirate Ship' was still open for business. She had originally been built as a Swedish coastal trading ketch but came to Essex waters as a charter vessel around 1973. By 1976 she was put up for sale at Portsmouth and re-rigged as a double topsail schooner. Subsequently she arrived at Binfield on the Medina and became decked out as a tourist attraction pirate ship, moving to various Newport Harbour berths over the next few years. A steady decline due to age and lack of water integrity got the better of her several years ago. Beyond lies the *Ash Lake* also briefly open to the public and similarly on borrowed time.

113. BALLASTER and SOU'WESTER

The dredging lighter *Ballaster* sits in the foreground whilst beyond lies the large white hulled motor yacht *Sou'wester*. The image dates from c1975 when the upper berths at Newport Harbour had already been largely forsaken by regular trading vessels. St. Thomas' Church can be seen distant above the new dual carriageway bridge which replaced the railway viaduct and bridge. Newport Gasworks had been situated behind the trees off to the left. The Model Store, right, has yet to be touched.

114. BOLGEN →

Looking very smart is the privately owned ex Danish coaster *Bolgen* 72grt./1902. She had been in local Solent waters for many years as a motor yacht. The image is included to show the dwellings development across the river where the Model Store stood. The May 2003 image appears remarkably clear of land placed yachts in lay-up. The last cargo day boats departed some twenty years earlier.

115. PS Monarch passing Odessa Shipyard →

The little paddler is seen here in 2008 heading upstream to the 'head of navigation' by the Quay Arts complex on a special inaugural trip for the I.O.W. Walking Festival. The shipyard slipway lies beyond other craft behind *Monarch's* funnel. The sharp eyed may observe the Island's High Sheriff for the year, Mr.Alan Titchmarsh standing next to the after saloon on the ship, about to officially launch the Festival. The cottage at the Odessa Yard is freshly painted and now stands totally surrounded by modern industrial activity. Long gone are the fields and countryside thereabouts.

mg heating

116. CELTIC

The 153grt./1903 built *Celtic*, once one of the dozen or so Dutch built steel hulled spritsail sailing barges described earlier in the book (see no.52) has recently retired from the bagged cement trade in this 1969 image. This ship had lost her sailing rig in deference to motor power and modernisation in 1941 when twin motors and screws were fitted. This operation enabled many an ancient hull to compete with newer ships. *Celtic* often lifted 200 ton cement cargoes from Asham on the River Ouse in Sussex to Newport for her owner Capt. Sheaf. Once his new vessel *Ash Lake* entered service the old *Celtic* went to the Thames for further work, but ended up at the Dolphin Sailing Barge Museum at Sittingbourne.

117. CELTIC at Sittingbourne →

In this September 2005 photograph at Sittingbourne things looked bleak for the old barge as attempts to alter her wheelhouse and after deck had ground to a halt as the project ceased momentum. The protective hoops over to the right stand over the hull of the well known ex Everard sailing barge *Cambria* – she never became motorised and carried her last commercial cargo under sail alone in 1971. Having also suffered many a restoration setback, this barge has recently been put back under sail in full working order after a near total rebuild. No such luck for the *Celtic*.

CELTIC

118. Newport Harbour in 2011
The harbour has now been largely abandoned by commercial trade and yachts have taken over most moorings and quaysides. The Jubilee Stores serves on as offices and beyond, the white building now houses the popular Vintage Bus Museum.

JUBILEE STORES
STUDIOS

119. TS CAROLINE ALLEN

Photographed in May 2010 during Newport's 'Riverfest' is the miniature square rigged training ship *Caroline Allen*. The bunting and shiny funnel in the foreground belong to one of the event-attending steam launches.

120. TS BOB ALLEN

On the same date the identical sister vessel is moored close to the Bargeman's Rest pub. Above, minus only its stout brick chimney lies the remains of Newport's first electric power station, forlornly abandoned. It dates from c1900.

121. SS LECONFIELD

With demolition all around on a misty melancholy morning in 1973, destruction in abundance was occurring as railway and much harbour side infrastructure came under attack, due to changing circumstances and modernisation. To add to this, two vessels await demolition:- 1. SS *Leconfield* 91grt./1936, and 2. the *Hatfield*, whose bow is just visible far left. Once the pride and joy of Littlehampton Harbour Commissioners, the steam grab dredger had put in a few further years working in the Solent area. In the gloom beyond, a gap exists where the railway viaduct stood, now permitting a temporary view of the houses in Sea Street. To the left a mound of chalk is growing in readiness for construction of the new dual carriageway embankment and bridge in much the same spot the old railway bridge occupied.

← 122. The Derrick Store

Once another of Newport Quay's well known warehouses, a large wooden derrick stood between the quayside and the building. Cargo could be lifted straight out of the barge holds across the public road directly into the store. Minus its boom the upright part can be seen in this 1973 photograph apparently rising out of *Leconfield's* wheelhouse. More chalk is arriving and beyond in the mist lies the site of Newport's once extensive junction railway station, engine sheds and goods yard. The railway closed here at the end of 1966 some one hundred and four years after it opened for the Cowes and Newport Railway Company.

123. The Bargeman's Rest Pub in 2011

The now well known pub has extended to left and right of the old Derrick store building. The derrick itself has survived the turmoil over the years and shows up here in white seemingly protruding from a large catamaran cabin cruiser perched on the quayside. The poor old derelict power station has a giant new plastic neighbour.

124. Newport Railway Bridge

The brick constructed bridge carried two separate lines over the Medina. The furthest from the camera and the last in service (1966) was the Cowes-Newport-Ryde line. Closest, the Newport-Sandown branch had closed in 1956, and already lost its spans in this view. The opening mechanism to allow tall masted ships to pass to upper wharves was unusual. It involved raising and side rolling of the two individual track spans by way of cams, gears, rollers and serious manpower, to the west (Newport Station) side of the opening. There were many heated disputes between the railway operators and barge crews over delays to opening the bridge for shipping. No doubt the railway's once meticulous adherence to operating timetables did not help a lot. When the railway closed in 1966, the problem simply vanished for ever.

125. The Bridge and RIVERCLOSE →

Moored up against the bridge abutment is Vectis Shippings' motor barge *Riverclose* 110grt./1957, and one of four similar craft built between 1954 and 1962. (see also *Murius*). The view dates from not long after closure of the Ryde line as it too shows just one girder span in situ.

126. Newport's dual carriageway bridge c1985

By this time the upper reaches of Newport Harbour had very much retired from trade. No provision had to be made for the passage of tall masted vessels! The black painted propeller on a plinth belonged to the old wooden trawler *Yellowfin* which ended its days around these parts. One modern link with the past does however survive - an Alan Shepard "Carrier & Removal" van is about to cross the little access bridge to the narrowing Medina river.

5. The Brewing Industry

Brew houses were established in the 1600s and one at Brading sold much beer to the fleet anchored in St. Helens Roads. By 1643 Mew, Langton's Brewery at Newport was shipping beer down river to Cowes for export. The Company supplied large quantities of beer to ships calling off Cowes at the start of their lengthy overseas voyages. The Mew, Langton Company were the innovators of screw topped beer containers – the first in the World – in the late 1800s. These were said to be urgently required to eliminate excessive breakage of glass bottles containing India Pale Ale supplied for the troops out in India.

127. River Medina 'head of navigation'

The view from beneath the modern road bridge in 2011 shows the very top of Newport's once bustling commercial harbour. On the right are buildings now used by Quay Arts which in a previous life had been the main departure point for beer brewed by Mew, Langton at Crocker Street a few hundred yards off to the west. The Lukely Brook joins the Medina in this corner of the harbour on its journey from the Carisbrooke area. That waterway was once navigable by small barges to the Crocker Street brewery. Barrels brought downstream were lifted onto the wall from the boats, thence transported around the corner to the main barge berth for loading and onward transit. A narrow gauge railtrack and trolleys provided the method to by-pass the sill/sluice arrangement where the stream entered the harbour proper. Also visible here to the left is the exit channel for the main river Medina, much reduced in volume at this point, the tide barely rises at all just a few hundred yards to the South. Distant in the centre of town stands the tower of Newport Minster.

128. XXXX

Deliberately included here is a photograph of the White's built beer barge *XXXX* of 1948, seen motoring further down the river. This was the second of two motor barges that Mew, Langton used to carry their own cargoes to and from their Mainland Solent terminals. The earlier barge had been the *Wight* 57grt/1921, with Lymington and Southampton the destinations. Brickwoods, shipped their beers to a terminal at Wootton Bridge from their Portsmouth Brewery.

129. The Medina's upper reaches →

This photograph dates from the late 1950s and is typical of how old industrial areas were 'ripening' for modern development and renewal. The warehouses here handled much sack type traffic, and their fronts faced out onto Sea Street. The Medina here had been severely pinched by the construction of the viaduct essential for the Sandown railway line to reach into Newport Station in 1882. Shepard Brothers' tiny motor barge *SBL 6*, 37grt./1925 sits aground at low water. She measured just 60ft loa and 14ft beam. The Medina is thought to have been navigable a couple of centuries earlier to as far as the foot of Pyle Street. Even earlier a ford type river crossing at Shide may have been the highest limit for small craft, before any bridges were built nearer to Newport.

130. Crouchers' steam wagon and warehouse →

In conjunction with the operation of their own barge fleet, the firm made deliveries around the Island by road. Posing outside their warehouse is a fine example of a steam road wagon and trailer. Sitting on the steam wagon is one of the early wooden almost 'universal' containers which fitted equally well onto rail wagons, barge holds or even horse drawn carts. They were in reality the fore runners of the modern containers we are so familiar with today. The image pre-dates WW1 – well before the proliferation of the internal combustion engined van and lorry.

CROUCHERS LTD.
AILWAY & GENERAL
CARRIERS.
REMOVAL
ONTRACTORS
REMOVAL CONTRACTORS.
CROUCHERS LTD.
NEWPORT, SOUTHAMPTON,
PORTSMOUTH & COWES.
SHIPPING & FORWARDING AGENTS
CROUCHERS LTD.
HOUSEHOLD REMOVALS &
WAREHOUSING ESTIMATES FREE
NEWPORT, I.W.
CROUCHERS LTD.
FURNITURE REMOVERS

Map No. 6 Newport-Wootton-Ryde

(1) Hurstake (old shipyard)
(2) West Medina Mill – (corn, thence cement)
(3) East Medina Mill (corn)
(4) Wootton Bridge Mill (corn)
(5) Fishbourne – the ultimate site for the car ferry terminal in 1927
(6) Quarr Abbey to Binstead (early stone quarry sites).

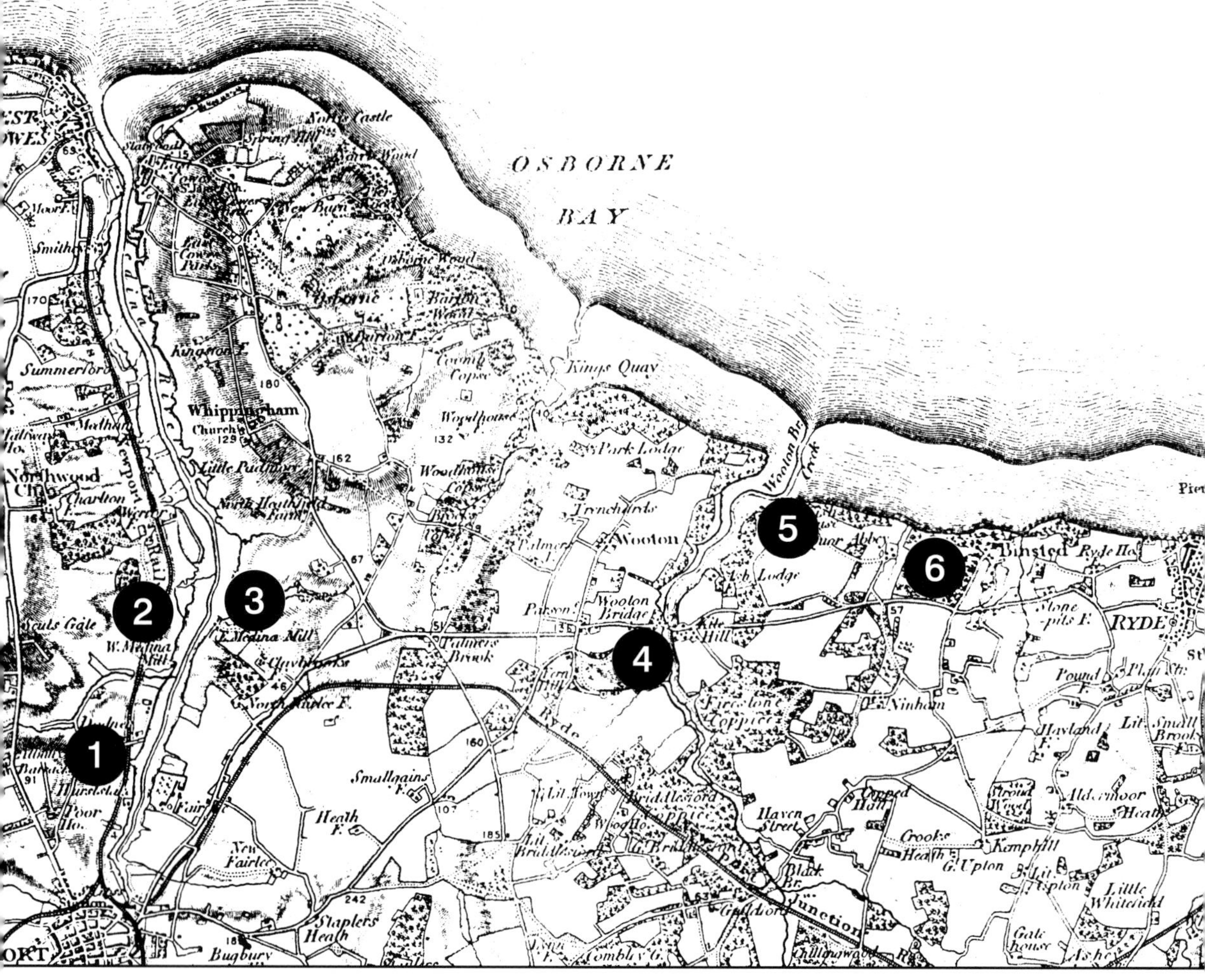

131. Newport Reform Wharf (memorial tablet)

Inserted in a section of parapet wall at Newport's Coppins Bridge is an engraved stone tablet, now much faded. It commemorates the year 1832 when the Corporation granted a piece of land to the Church for 1/- (one shilling) per year for thirty years, for the benefit of the poor. The Reform Wharf was situated between Coppins Bridge and Tucker's Coal Wharf. Photograph 2011.

132. SILENT at Wootton Mill

The mill pond across the road could be filled at every high tide by way of sluices under the roadway. The water would then be released as required to power the mill which did a brisk trade with the mainland. The large mill building stood adjacent to the bridge and creek from around 1700 until demolition in 1962. The current Sloop Inn once served as the miller's dwelling. This delightful image from the 1900s shows no less than three local trading ketches attending the Mill. Bow on to the camera is the most regular visiting vessel *Silent* 19reg.tons/1860 and she still traded for Souters of Wootton Mill into the 1930s, often to and from Southampton with grain. The mill also had steam power as a tall metal chimney has appeared. The road has been widened now for modern traffic but sluices are still required to scour the channel on the ebb tide. Quarr Monastery established an embankment and mill here as early as the 1100s.

133. HILSEA at Fishbourne

The first berth at Fishbourne on Wootton Creek opened by the Southern Railway in 1925 initially took the tug and tow-boat traffic away from Ryde Esplanade where at low water, the site would dry out for hours between successive high tides. The first of the revolutionary purpose built ferries, *Fishbourne* entered service on the new route in 1927, to be followed by *Wootton* in 1928 and the final ship photographed here in 1930. The berth was built at ninety degrees to the creek shore line but at 149grt and just 131ft loa, the ships would have little difficulty in so manoeuvring. They were fitted with four propellers and four rudders and could muster 240hp giving a speed of 8kts with a journey time of 55 minutes from Broad Street, Portsmouth. Depending on car size some 16 to 20 could be carried.

134. FISHBOURNE (1) →

Seen here in her original guise is the first of the trio from 1927. *Fishbourne* 136grt was powered by two sets of semi-diesel engines built by Norris, Henty and Gardner. The Southern employed their most favoured regular conventional ferry builder - Denny's of Dumbarton - to construct this new class of vessel. *Fishbourne* and *Wootton* both assisted in the evacuation of Dunkirk in 1940.

135. FISHBOURNE (2) →

Car traffic grew steadily post WW2 and by the late 1950s some consideration just had to be given to the replacement of the thirty year old little ships on the route. The second *Fishbourne* seen here in later British Rail 'Sealink' livery entered service in 1961, and could carry 34 cars at 10kts giving a journey time closer to 35 minutes. This new generation of ferries had the advanced Voith-Schneider propulsion units first trialled successfully on *Lymington* in 1938. Berth improvements were made at Broad Street and Fishbourne, where a ninety degree turn was eliminated by aligning the new berth with Wootton Creek's approach channel.

Sealink

136. CAMBER QUEEN

Seen arriving at the new berth in 1969 at low water is another 1961 entrant to the service. At this period the berthing pier lay to the west of the concrete slip-way ramp arrangement.

137. CUTHRED at sea →

The first of a third generation ferry appeared in 1969. The overall increase in all types of traffic volume over the previous ten years necessitated quick remedial action. This new class, led by *Cuthred* 704grt, would be joined by improved sister vessels *Caedmon, Cenwulf* and *Cenred* by 1973, the latter pair destined for the Lymington-Yarmouth route. These ships carried 750 passengers and some 52 cars. *Caedmon* later also joined the Lymington-Yarmouth service, whilst *Cuthred* was withdrawn in 1986. The remaining three were duly fitted with lifting upper car decks to further increase capacity.

138. Fishbourne Slipway in 1969 →

Making the final approach to the berth on Wootton creek, the new *Cuthred* appears lightly laden with cars and a couple of vans. It would be the coming decade of the 1970s that would see a vast increase in commercial traffic as the little day-boat general cargo barges were losing their hold on cross-Solent goods transport. Door to door commercial deliveries made it imperative for a yet larger class of ferry to be brought into service. Broad Street Terminal at Portsmouth had also reached full capacity so with the Royal Navy shrinking, the newly available and larger Gun Wharf site was selected for the future ferry terminal. This purpose built terminal could cope with vastly larger car and truck numbers and opened in 1982. Similar berth improvements and general terminal enlargements were carried out at Fishbourne.

139. ST. CATHERINE

In 1983 the first new 'superferry' for the route entered service under the 'Sealink' banner. The largest yet on any IOW route at 2,036grt., 250 ft.loa by 55ft. beam some 142 cars could be carried or with a reduced car capacity to accommodate several of the now commonplace articulated trailer trucks. This generation of ship did however revert to traditional bow and stern arrangements with the bridge at the forward end of the accommodation block. With drive through ability, this necessitates turning the ships through one hundred and eighty degrees off each berth. Generally ships berth stern to the ramp at Gun Wharf and proceed bow first into Wootton Creek for the Fishbourne Terminal. In the 1983 photograph *St.Catherine* has an interim plain red funnel awaiting British Rail Sealink's 1984 privatisation.

140. ST. HELEN (Sealink Livery) →

Seen just berthing to the new 'east side' pier at Fishbourne is the second of the new Saint class vessels to enter service in 1983. She carries the new privatised Sealink British Ferries livery, thus ending the Railways' tradition of operating passenger and car ferries to the Island.

141. Wightlink livery →

Another view of *St.Catherine* showing off a new colour scheme in morning sunshine at Fishbourne in 2004. The ship became surplus to requirements in 2010 and went out to the Mediterranean for further service in Sardinian waters.

BRITISH
FERRIES

ST. CATHERINE
LONDON

142. ST. CLARE at Portsmouth Harbour 2012 →

Still more traffic growth on the route, especially freight units making Island deliveries generally, would necessitate the introduction of one further even larger ferry. This duly appeared in the guise of the Polish built *St.Clare* 5,349grt./ 2001. Capable of carrying 900 passengers and up to 204 cars this ship reverted to the earlier true reversible double-ended design, thereby eliminating turning round off the berths entirely. An innovation would see a permanently fixed upper car deck at a greater height above the maindeck to accommodate the large commercial vehicles below. In this photograph the ship is in the latest Wightlink livery.

6. Stone Quarrying

The limestone quarries just to the east of Quarr Abbey near to Binstead had been in use since the 1100s and probably worked even earlier, variously by the Romans and Saxons. In the Norman period the stone was much in demand for church and cathedral building projects on the nearby mainland. The best quality stone is thought to have been worked out by the 1300s although lesser quality material continued to be extracted until around 1850. Bembridge limestone was also quarried and shipped out long ago. Chalk from the Downs was extracted in many locations for agricultural use and as already described for cement manufacture.

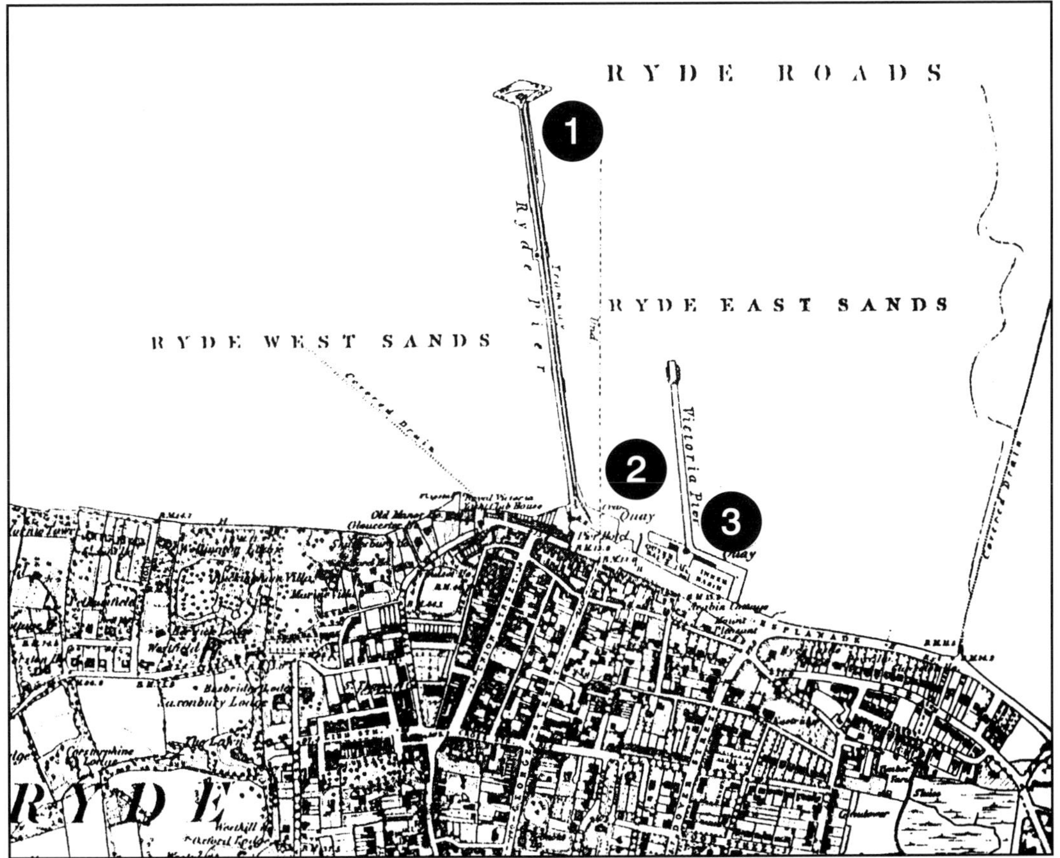

Map No. 7 Ryde Piers and Basins

(1) Ryde Pier Head c1865 – walkway and tramway only, pre railway era

(2) George Street Slipway (tow-boat landing place)

(3) Inner and Outer Basins and Victoria Pier.

7. General Goods in Transit

Two Island families established services to and from the mainland by around the year 1800. Shepard's first vessel the *Good Intent*, was believed to have been built at Hurstake, Newport as early as 1780. Two ships were trading to London from Newport and Cowes on a weekly frequency in 1832. Crouchers' fleet expanded too, in the latter 1800s and their ship naming system became something of a tradition – fox hunting terminology – this method of nomenclature lasting for one hundred years. By the 1860s Pickfords were operating Portsmouth-Ryde-Cowes services as in 1862 they had become agents for the London, Brighton and South Coast Railway Company. The main general trading ports were Newport, Cowes, Portsmouth and Southampton with Ryde, St. Helens and Yarmouth used by some operators. Wootton maintained a regular service to Portsmouth until the 1870s.

Crouchers' vessels received goods directly from ocean going ships at Southampton and also transported timber unloaded from steamers at Medham moorings on the Medina, South of Cowes. By the late 1800s Chaplins were also involved in cross-Solent movement of goods often to Ryde and St. Helens

143. Unloading at Ryde Sands

This delightful image, seen courtesy of the Isle of Wight Heritage Service, is taken from an 1830 painting by A.V.C. Fielding. The vessel shown is a small local sailing ketch trader with a surprisingly ornate stern design. She is unloading to the two-horse cart waiting on the sands and they have turned the cart ready for the 'off'. This time honoured operation took place, tide and weather permitting, right around the UK shoreline where practicable. As ships grew larger and cargoes more valuable proper protected wharves, jetties and quays became necessary to allay increasing insurance costs.

quays. Pickfords absorbed many smaller operators in 1936 thus forming a twenty one ship fleet. Cowes became the main general goods receiving port and Newport tended towards the handling of bulk cargoes and the beer trade. Many of the long serving wooden hulled motor barges – often upgraded sailing types – were replaced after WW2 with larger capacity vessels. The earlier small dimension wooden containers were capable of carriage by ship, barge, rail or road wagon. Just after WW2 when the nationalisation 'fad' was at its greatest, all such services involving sea and road transport locally were placed under the ownership of the British Transport Commission. In 1956 this altered to British Road Services whose name quickly appeared on barge sides.

The last motor barge built to serve the Island with general goods on a daily basis was the *Northwood* 171grt./1962, and she almost ranked as a full sized coaster in comparison to the 25 to 50grt vessels of but a decade earlier. The day service to Point Wharf, Portsmouth ended in 1975 and *Northwood* was put up for sale.

144. The first Ryde Pier

A postcard image, but from an earlier unknown source, this drawing shows the original wooden short length pier built in 1814. Even so, it reached out some 1,250ft into slightly deeper water to where a single set of steps completed the end. Various small craft are scattered about and a very early wooden hulled paddler lays off the pier. One of the earliest Solent area steamers was reportedly the *Prince Coburg* in 1820. By 1824 other local steamers were operating and it became necessary to lengthen the pier no less than three times between 1815 and 1833, eventually to 2,250ft. Proper pierhead steamer berths arrived in 1842 and had to be enlarged as soon as 1859. Next came the parallel tramway pier in 1862/3, reconstructed in 1886. The third pier, parallel to the others arrived in 1879/80 courtesy of the railway companies.

145. Ryde Pier, Paddler and Tow-boat in 1831

Another splendid image from the local Brannon collection, Ryde Pier had by now been extended with a slightly larger berth for a steamer. Ryde town appears quite well built up and expanding and the paddler could well be one of the following: *Union* b.1822, *Lord Yarborough* b.1826 or the *Arrow* of 1823 when four sailings per day excepting Sundays operated. PS *George IV* made a weekly foray cross Channel to Le Havre. The 'horse' or 'tow-boat' astern of the paddler has a rather classy looking carriage onboard complete with two horses ready for the shore. The boat would be brought inshore to the George Street slipway for disembarkation to the relief no doubt of all concerned.

146. The 'Port of Ryde' c1870s. →

There were small basins, tidal in nature, along the Esplanade before the arrival of the Railway here in 1880 from the already operational Ryde St. Johns Station. Several interesting small trading vessels can be seen alongside, the nearest of which is the Cowes built *Dove* 17reg./1820, a smack type. Beyond lies a topsail schooner and although it is difficult to precisely date the scene, no railway pier is evident in the background. In 1872 the *Dove* was registered as owned by Thomas Holbrook of Newtown.

147. The Esplanade c1870s. →

Sadly a poorer image yet fascinating as it shows Hackney carriages waiting in the foreground. The little dock basins exhibit a number of sailing craft masts pointing skywards, and the outline of the 1864 Victoria Pleasure Pier is just visible.

TRANSIT RYDE

148. ASTEROID at Ryde Esplanade wall

The buildings opposite are little altered today in 2012 compared to this image from around 1890-1900. The iron railings each side of the railway track's descent to the tunnel can be clearly seen. There are horse drawn vans in attendance belonging to Curtiss & Co., and Peacocks and a great variety of bagged, baled, barrelled and boxed goods unloaded for Island destinations. Chaplin & Co's little wooden trading ketch *Asteroid* 24reg./1884 has a traditional simple gaff and tackle rigged for cargo work. There were no cranes hereabouts. This so called 'port' location was very exposed to Northerly winds and dried out twice a day for hundreds of yards at low water. However, and no doubt for local convenience reasons, vessels were still being unloaded by horses and carts on Ryde sands between WW1 and WW2.

149. Victoria Pier (c1890s) →

Another difficult image to precisely date, this pier seems to have been rarely photographed. It first appeared in 1859 to be rebuilt in final form by 1864 and would only reach to about half the length of its grander, more useful neighbour. It was reportedly none too successful a venture as proper regular steamer services could not be attracted because of Ryde sands. It was derelict by WW1 and had succumbed to total demolition by 1922.

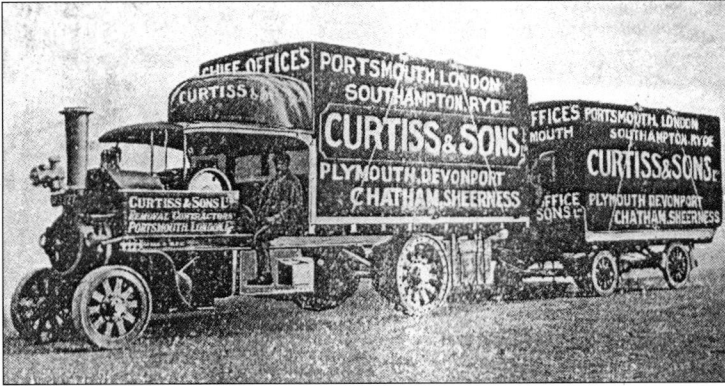

ARE YOU REMOVING?
WRITE FOR ESTIMATE TO

CURTISS & SONS, LTD.

DEPOSITORIES.

PORTSMOUTH	..	Royal Pantechnicon
PORTSEA ..	..	The Hard (adjoining Harbour Station)
LONDON ..	..	28, Farringdon St., E.C.
GOSPORT ..	..	60, High Street
SOUTHAMPTON	..	28, Queen's Terrace
RYDE	..	1, Esplanade
PLYMOUTH ..	..	121, Tavistock Road
DEVONPORT ..	..	46-9, Chapel Street
CHATHAM ..	..	351, High St., Rochester
SHEERNESS ..	..	72, High St., Blue Town
HAVANT ..	..	Railway Stn. (adjoining)
BOURNEMOUTH	..	180, Holdenhurst Road

Chief Offices—
Royal Pantechnicon, Portsmouth.
FURNITURE, &c., WAREHOUSED.

150. The final version of Ryde Pier

Probably taken in the 1920s the image shows a train of four wheeled 'bouncer' carriages having trundled down the Pier to the Esplanade Station, leaving another issuing steam at Pierhead to follow. One of Chaplins' motor barges lies close to the shore beyond a hand crane. Today the area off to the right forms the modern Hoverport.

151. ASTEROID (motorised) →

This image is seen courtesy of Carisbrooke Castle Museum and the 1884 built graceful sailing ketch has been cut down to motor barge rig by her owners, Chaplins. The cargo boom would now no doubt be left permanently rigged for action and a tiny wind break shelter has appeared aft at the conning position – far short of wheelhouse protection! Two of the joint LB&SC Railway and L&SW Railway paddle steamers are berthed at the pier head and one of His Majesty's finest sits at anchor out in Spithead. (c1920).

152. JJC on Ryde Sands →

This scene compares interestingly with practices already described in the 1830 image. *JJC* 36grt./1910 came under Portsmouth registry and the ownership of John J. C. Stephens in 1925. Steel hulled and Dutch built, the image confirms such unloading work continued between the Wars hereabouts. Another vessel's mast can be seen beyond, and a second horse and cart round on the starboard side of the ship would help to concentrate minds and shovels before the incoming tidal invasion. Looking at wagon wheel marks in the sand the old horse's day is as yet far from done.

CHAPLIN&Co.
ASTEROID

ESTABLISHED 1846

FRASER & WHITE LTD F.I.C.S.

STEAMSHIP, TUG, BARGE & LIGHTER OWNERS

COAL MERCHANTS & FACTORS, SHIPBROKERS,
STEVEDORES, WAREHOUSEMEN & HAULAGE CONTRACTORS

PROMPT & EXPEDITIOUS HANDLING OF CARGOES & CUSTOMS BUSINESS

Agents for the P. & O. AND ALL THE PRINCIPAL STEAMSHIP LINES

This Silo at Portsmouth is constructed of ferro-concrete on the Kahncrete principle and has a capacity of 12.000 tons. The discharging plant was supplied by Messrs Sir William Arrol & Co. Ltd. of Glasgow and is designed to handle over 300 tons per hour. The transporters, as can be seen, are of the travelling type, and two vessels can be dealt with simultaneously.

OFFICES, WHARVES & DEPOTS AT —

PORTSMOUTH, COWES I.W., GOSPORT, FAREHAM, LYMINGTON Etc.

HEAD OFFICE:—

23 East Street, Town Quay, PORTSMOUTH, ENG.

LLOYDS AGENT, PORTSMOUTH (H. D. GILBERT)

COWES I.W. Office–Fountain Yard. Phone:- 177 Cowes, Telegrams:- Fraser, Cowes

BUNKER COAL & FRESH WATER SUPPLIED AT SHORTEST NOTICE

STEAM TUGS ALWAYS AVAILABLE

8. Early Passenger Services

The Island's population numerically would have been fairly static until the coming of steamships and railways. The first paddle steamers arrived in the Solent area around 1820, two decades before railway lines were built in Hampshire or Sussex.

IOW populations were:-

1801	22,000
1861	55,000
1971	110,000
2011	132,000

At Lymington (for Yarmouth), the Lymington Railway Company arrived in 1858
At Southampton (for Cowes), the London & Southampton Railway " " 1840
At Portsmouth (for Ryde), the London, Brighton & South Coast Railway " 1847

Intending cross-Solent passengers in the pre steam era were reliant on sailing wherries totally dependent on wind, tide and the boatmen involved. Landings would have been principally within the sheltered river estuaries, harbours and creeks although the beaches too played their part. The construction of Ryde Pier, one of the earliest to be built anywhere in 1814, would soon permit the first tiny wooden paddle steamers to disgorge their passengers to a purpose built structure. This happened at Ryde shortly before 1820 and a steamer was running from Southampton to Cowes around the same date. PS *Glasgow* 17reg.tons started on the Lymington-Yarmouth route before 1830. In 1840 the Solent Steam Packet Company was formed to specifically take advantage of the expected railway generated traffic of the future. In 1855 the Railway Companies took over that firm themselves. The Portsmouth-Ryde route had been served by the Portsmouth and Ryde Steam Packet Company in earlier days.

In 1845 Queen Victoria and Prince Albert chose Osborne House, East Cowes to be their favourite residential retreat and this alone brought about a vast increase in passenger and goods services as it so happily coincided with the rapid growth of the railway network. (1862 on the Island). The Island also became a regular stopping off point for a growing network of longer distance coastal passenger steamer routes. This traffic would ultimately be lost entirely to the railways.

153. PS PORTSDOWN

When this smart looking steamer and sister vessel *Merstone* both 342grt./1928 arrived on the Portsmouth-Ryde service they represented a large improvement in design and comfort compared to their predecessors. This included much increased enclosed passenger accommodation and a proper enclosed wheelhouse for the Master, Officer of the Watch, and the helmsman. *Portsdown's* career sadly ended early when she struck a mine and sank quickly off Southsea in 1941. *Merstone* went for scrap in 1952.

154. MV SHANKLIN →

Seen running parallel to the Southsea shore in 1952 is the almost new motor ferry *Shanklin* 833grt./1951, the third of a trio designed to take over the duties of some of the last generation of paddle steamers on the Ryde Pier route. Far beamier than their predecessors they were at first regarded as not being quite such good 'sea boats'. The paddlers invariably had sharp bows and fine hull lines. The new ships were 200ft loa with a beam of 47.6ft but a good passenger carrying complement of up to 1,300 persons. They were real crowd shifters for the year round service and peak summer holiday loads. *Shanklin* was sold in 1980 to begin a new career in the Bristol Channel area as *Prince Ivanhoe* but became a total loss about a year later after a disagreement with an underwater obstacle off the Gower Peninsula. The next new generation of ferries for the route were to be the catamaran types *Our Lady Pamela* and *Our Lady Patricia* 313grt./ 1986 built in Tasmania. *Brading* went for scrap but the final survivor of the early motor trio *Southsea*, nearly made preservation status after years in lay-up variously at Falmouth, Newhaven and Southampton. The scrap man finally got his hands on her at a Continental scrap yard c2005.

155. SOUTHSEA and OUR LADY PATRICIA ↓

A 1988 view from the deck of a departing car ferry shows the veteran Portsmouth to Ryde passenger ferry *Southsea* 837grt./1948 in her final post railway 'Sealink' guise. The old ship was just completing her 40th season and went into lay-up directly. The stern of a newly arrived 'cat' can be seen at the Portsmouth Harbour Station berth, with a Gosport ferry and *HMS Warrior* in the background.

156. Wightlink's Portsmouth moorings

The photograph dates from 2002 and catching the evening sun are *St.Catherine*, one of the '*Fast Cats*', the bunkering tanker *Jaynee W.* 1,689grt./1986, with *Warrior's* masts above and *HMS Victory* further into the Dockyard. Several naval vessels lie alongside.

157. FASTCAT RYDE at sea →

The '*Our Lady*' cats were replaced around 1995 with a pair of vessels named *Fastcat Ryde* and *Fastcat Shanklin* 478grt, and able to carry 333 passengers each. Unusually the photograph shows the former in 2003 departing West Cowes on a temporary service for yachtsmen to Lymington during Cowes Week, that year. The striking yellow livery applied to these and the earlier cats would not be repeated on the third generation vessels.

158. FASTCAT RYDE at Ryde Pier Head in 2004 →

A far cry from the graceful paddlers of old disgorging thousands of folk every day onto Ryde Pier, today circumstances are somewhat different and the impression now created is of a commuters' car park. The electric powered baggage handling crane survives to remind one of old practices as the traditional ferries each had a large conventional hold and lifting hatch cover for the many GPO mail trolleys then in constant circulation. The modern catamarans are undoubtedly fast and efficient in their own way, but the naval architects seem unable to design attractive stern profiles – these areas seem more to resemble something seen on an allotment, or bike sheds.

fast CAT

www.wightlink.co.uk
astcat-Ryde
Portsmouth

159. Ryde Hoverport 2012

The buildings across the Esplanade make an interesting comparison with the much earlier *Asteroid* image (148). In this modern scene two of Hovertravel's current craft are up on the slipway. Nearest the camera is *Freedom Express* the most recent addition whilst beyond lies *Freedom 90*. The service to and from Southsea Beach Terminal commenced almost five decades ago and is now much appreciated by both tourists and regular commuters alike, and remains the world's only regular route to employ such craft.

160. WIGHT RYDER 1 →

Seen arriving just inside Portsmouth Harbour entrance in May 2012 is one of the latest pair of fast catamarans employed by Wightlink on the Portsmouth Harbour Station to Ryde Pier route. Dating from 2009 these vessels are a far cry from the traditional type of ferries once in service on this cross-Solent route. Speed and frequency of service are necessary today to shift the passenger numbers whereas the old ferries could manage about 1,000 souls per trip in virtually any weather.

SOUTHDOWN MOTOR SERVICES LTD.
(BOOKING AGENTS)

Nº 1761

A Pioneer Hovercraft Service
by WESTLAND SR·N2
between RYDE and SOUTHSEA
Date 21st August 1962 Time 5-25

single fare TEN SHILLINGS

Ticket for the trial service.

161. PS WAVERLEY ↓

En route for an afternoon cruise around Portsmouth Harbour in September 2007 is the much travelled preserved paddle steamer *Waverley*. The Ryde to Portsmouth route saw several twin funnelled paddlers serve in earlier times when the Joint Railway Companies' *Victoria* (1880s), *Duchess of Connaught* and *Duchess of Edinburgh* from 1884 appeared. The latter two had twin funnels unusually placed athwartships, not fore and aft!

162. TS ROYALIST

Groves and Gutteridge built this smart little training brig at Cowes in 1971. At 110 tons she was the first brig built in the UK for many decades. In the mid 1970s photograph she is motoring out of Portsmouth Harbour entrance with some Cadets aloft preparing to unfurl the sails. The ship is still very active today and may often be seen far away from her Solent base area.

163. The Spinnaker Tower 2005

Since we have just been looking at parts of the Island nearest to Portsmouth it seems appropriate to include some images of that port. The just completed Spinnaker Tower has proved to be a very popular tourist attraction, apart from marking the position of Portsmouth Harbour in general from many miles around the area. In this photograph one of the smaller refrigerated cargo ships that now serve Portsmouth's growing fresh fruit import trade is seen arriving. *Frio Vladivostok* 3,817grt./1997 is heading up to the commercial port beyond the Navy base.

164. VILLE

Caught at work delivering rock armour in the entrance to the harbour in May 2005 is the little 'rock hopper dropper' *Ville* 499grt./ 1985 engaged in beefing up the sea wall protection. This vessel will be familiar to Islanders as she 'built' the new little boat haven at Ventnor (see later photograph).

165. Lee-on-Solent Pier

One of the nearest local mainland piers, this charming structure opened in 1888 and attracted considerable tourist excursion traffic from the Island. Vessels from Ryde, Cowes, Portsmouth, Southsea, Southampton and Seaview visited Lee's developing resort facilities. The photograph dates from 1925 and the board above the entrance way states -

'The Golden Hall - tea-dancing - music'.

166. Seaview Pier →

More for promenading or boarding excursion steamers, this attractive structure dated from 1879-81 with the pier head being added in 1889. It was a suspension type of pier with four pairs of towers from which the decking hung off connecting cables. It was built by Francis Caws, and said to have partly utilised sections from Brunel's original Hungerford Bridge on the Thames. It also somewhat resembled Brighton's legendary early Chain Pier of 1823. At 900ft in length Seaview Pier became popular with the smaller excursion steamers and for Trinity House pilots' shore access when boarding or leaving the many merchant ships passing through Spithead. It met its end after a 1951 storm.

Barnsley Creek

Once navigable by small trading vessels this creek lay between Seaview and Springvale. The long since vanished creek allowed ships to visit a mill at Pondwell in the flour and grain trade pre 1800. In that year an embankment was constructed across the mouth of the creek which for a time permitted a salt production business to operate for just a couple of decades. Salt production reportedly ceased in 1819 when the estate was sold.

Map No.8 Brading Quay and Harbour in the late 1860s

(1) Goods only line to the Quay
(2) Trestle pier and railway siding
(3) Further pier and siding
(4) Evidence of nearby Roman activity - (Brading Roman Villa 2 miles distant).

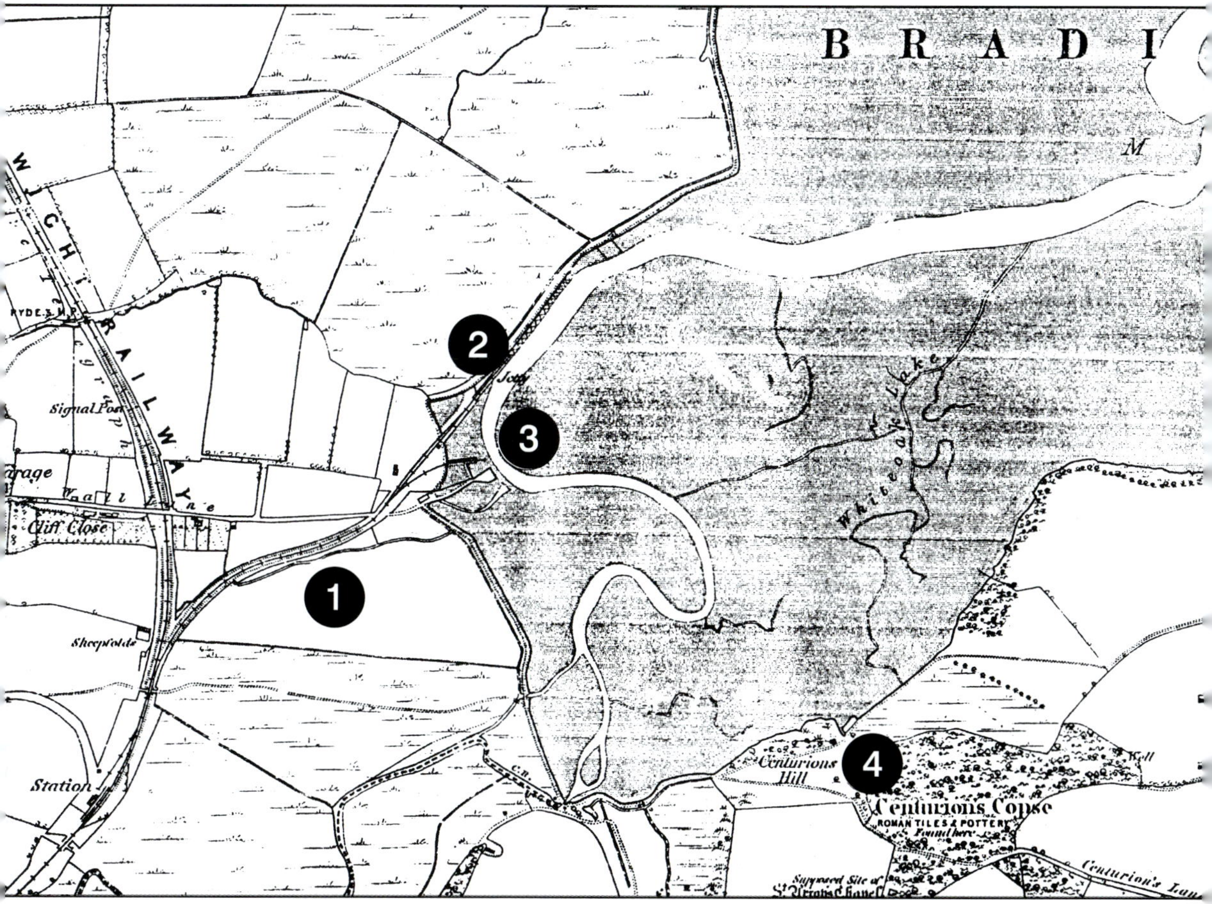

167. Brading Harbour

This once great shallow expanse extended almost to Brading Town from St. Helens and Bembridge. Given high water and suitable conditions in the twisting River Yar channels, vessels of some 150 tons capacity could reach Brading Quays. The Romans certainly saw the advantage of this sheltered inlet in order to serve their local interests at Brading Villa. By the 1600s ships were trading here with coal and grain. This splendid image has appeared many times over the years and curiously almost dates itself since the Ryde-Sandown railway line is present. Brading Station, just off to the right opened in 1864, whilst the new goods only line to the quay appearing pristine white, opened in 1865. A run-around facility for engines allowed goods trucks to be pushed out onto the trestle pier, just visible with the masts of a trading ketch alongside. Further sidings were later added. In 1874 the Brading Harbour Improvement Railway and Works Company began to extend the line towards St.Helens, and ultimately Bembridge which were reached in 1879 and 1882 respectively. A cement works opened at Brading in the mid 1800s, closed around 1900 only to re-open briefly between WW1 and WW2. The railway from Brading to Bembridge closed in 1953.

168. Brading Harbour and fields in 2011 →

This attempt to recapture the vista seen in the 1870s image has only been partially successful due to much tree encroachment in the area generally. Brading Church, visible far left, makes a good base point. Far distant left can be seen an extended St. Helens, (Bembridge is on the extreme right). Ships can be seen out in St.Helens anchorage beyond. The once great expanse of Brading Harbour is now rich agricultural meadow land and Brading Quay itself is lost from view.

169. ALFRED at St. Helens Mill →

The large tide mill had been at work here since 1780. Seen alongside with cargo gaff rigged is the little trading smack *Alfred* 19reg.tons/1835. The photograph is not easy to date but certainly seems well before 1900 when in that year the little ship was owned by Edward Way of Newport. Amazingly close examination of the image shows no less than ten characters posing for the photograph, in doorways, on the quay, on the ship etc; no doubt something out of the ordinary routine and a brief respite from coal or grain sack heaving! *Alfred* will be going nowhere for six hours – or at least until high water. The mill pond waters can be seen racing from the sluice just astern of the vessel.

170. SS ALLERWASH

Probably photographed before 1900, captured here is a veteran survivor of the coastal coal trade, the *Allerwash* 381grt./1861. An old iron hulled steamer lengthened in 1876 she traded on until the 1920s. The ship had an almost ridiculously tall funnel and still carried sails on what amounted to a schooner mast arrangement. St. Helens Quay suddenly grew in importance once Brading Harbour had been reclaimed, and the railway embankment built from Brading to Bembridge. The harbour reduced in size to the present 'Bembridge Harbour' status, would have been specially dredged to permit larger ships to reach St. Helens Quays, Gasworks and Mill. Also the brief but largely unsuccessful goods wagon train ferry from Langstone Harbour operated to St. Helens spasmodically, it is believed, between 1884-1888. That concern had been started by the IOW Marine Transit Company, later to be taken over by the LB&SCR who speedily forgot about it as fast as they could! The incumbent steamer PS *Carrier* 243grt./1858 had previously worked across the River Tay in Scotland. (see Solent-Creeks, Craft & Cargoes book for more information on that service).

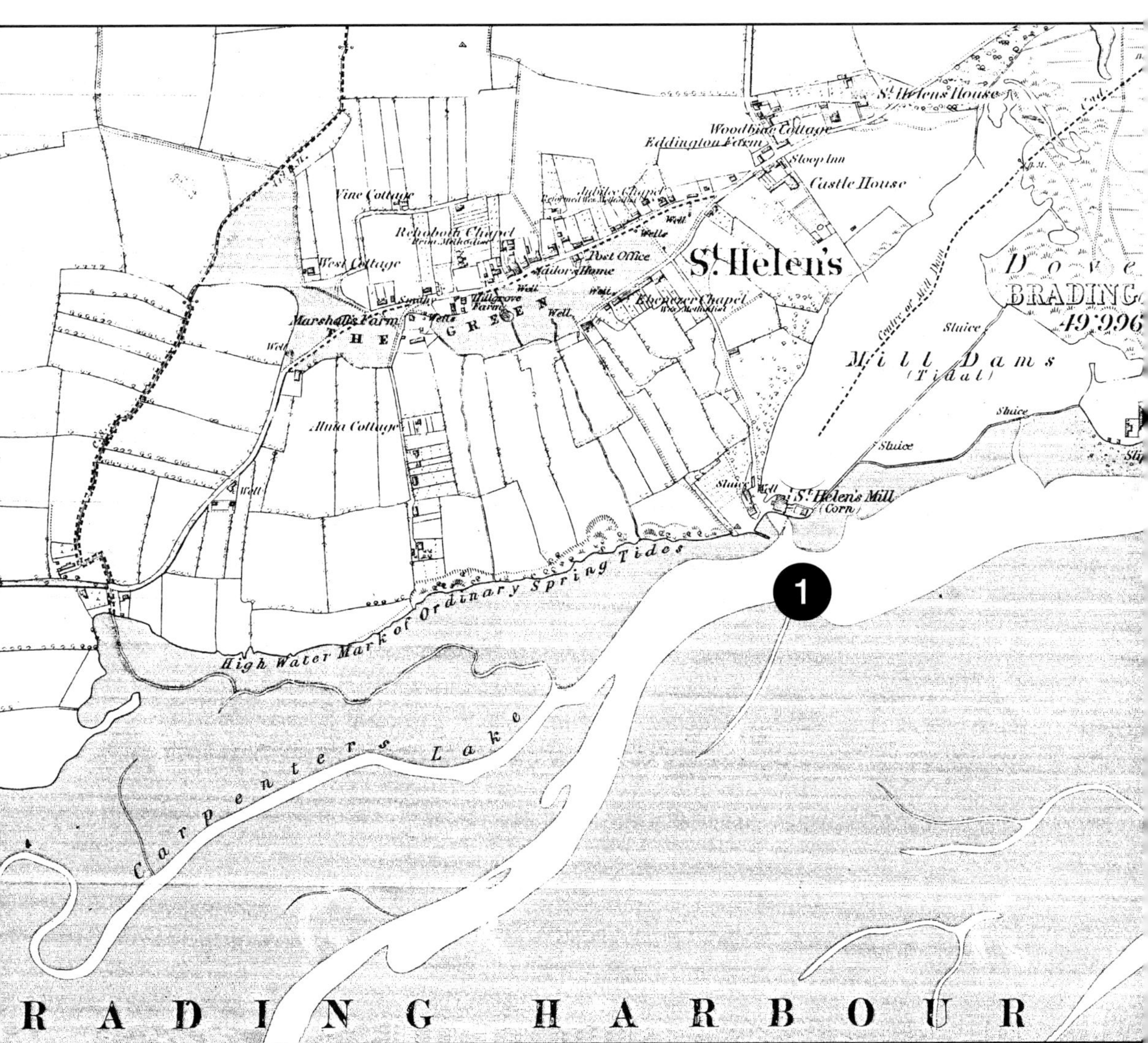

Map No. 9 Brading Harbour (E)

(1) St. Helens Tide Mill and ponds (corn).

171. Two Spritsail Barges, Bembridge Harbour 1924

This image is seen courtesy of Carisbrooke Castle Museum and shows a deeply laden barge under sail just picking up a tow for the inward journey to St. Helens Quays. The other outbound sailing barge is endeavouring to catch whatever wind it can to clear the harbour confines. The mizzen sail is yet to be set. Numerous patches on the nearer barge's sails are typical and indicate the 'make do and mend' philosophy of most sailing barge owners in trade. The two craft here were most likely in the local coal or grain distribution business. Brading Down is in the background.

172. WILBERNIA, EXCELSIOR and WILD SWAN →

The photograph is seen courtesy of the Isle of Wight Steam Railway archive and shows considerable activity c1930 at St. Helens Quays. There are no less than three interesting craft moored abreast, only clearly observed by a mast and derrick count! The small motor barge nearest the camera is the Chaplin operated *Wilbernia* 29grt, and Portsmouth built in 1923. The middle barge is *Wild Swan* 76grt./1913 a steel hulled motor barge built at Amsterdam. Alongside the quay is the tall funnelled steam barge *Excelsior* 66grt./1898 and built at Blackwall, on the Thames. Business must have been brisk from Portsmouth to the eastern Wight at this time. Various railway wagons beyond are exhibiting the fairly recent logo SR for Southern Railway, which appeared after the 1923 Railway Grouping arrangements. The warehouse also looks new.

173. Bembridge's new Lifeboat Station →

Photographed in January 2012 the newly constructed concrete pier and fine new lifeboat house at the seaward end, should see this busy station operational for many decades to come. Lifeboats have grown larger and more sophisticated ever since the first motor types were introduced. This has led to the rebuilding of many lifeboat houses around the UK and Irish coasts in recent years.

CHAPLINS LTD

Map. No.10 Bembridge Harbour

(1) New channel cut for the Eastern River Yar after land reclamation
(2) St. Helens Gasworks
(3) Still active corn mill (1930s)
(4) Site of the old train ferry berth (1880s)
(5) Bembridge Pier (pre WW1), and the Royal Spithead Hotel.

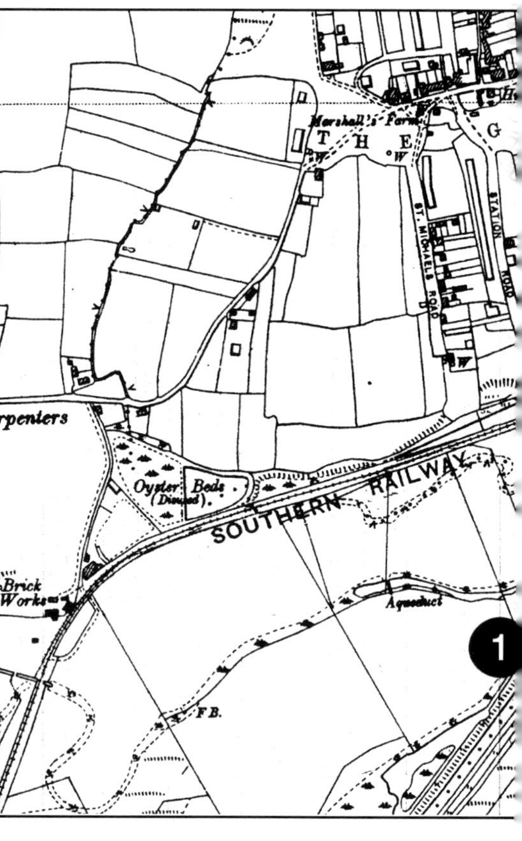

174. The 'Nab Tower to be'.

Seen completed at its Shoreham Harbour construction site c1919, is one of three anti-submarine defence structures originally destined for the narrow part of the Dover Strait during WW1. The war ended and towers two and three which were incomplete faced immediate demolition. The third tower seen here did have a future and was destined to be towed out by Admiralty tugs to be settled off the Nab Shoals as a permanent replacement for the Nab Lightship. So it remains to this day although now as an unmanned light tower and navigational mark, approaching its 100th birthday. The structure has had a slight lean ever since being settled onto the seabed.

175. Sandown → Pier and PS QUEEN

A calm summer's day c1930 and its not so busy at low tide with only a couple of white hulled rowing boats out on the water. Beyond, the paddle steamer *Queen* is setting off from the pier in a westerly direction on one of her 'Round the Island' trips. Sandown Pier dates from 1878 and survives today.

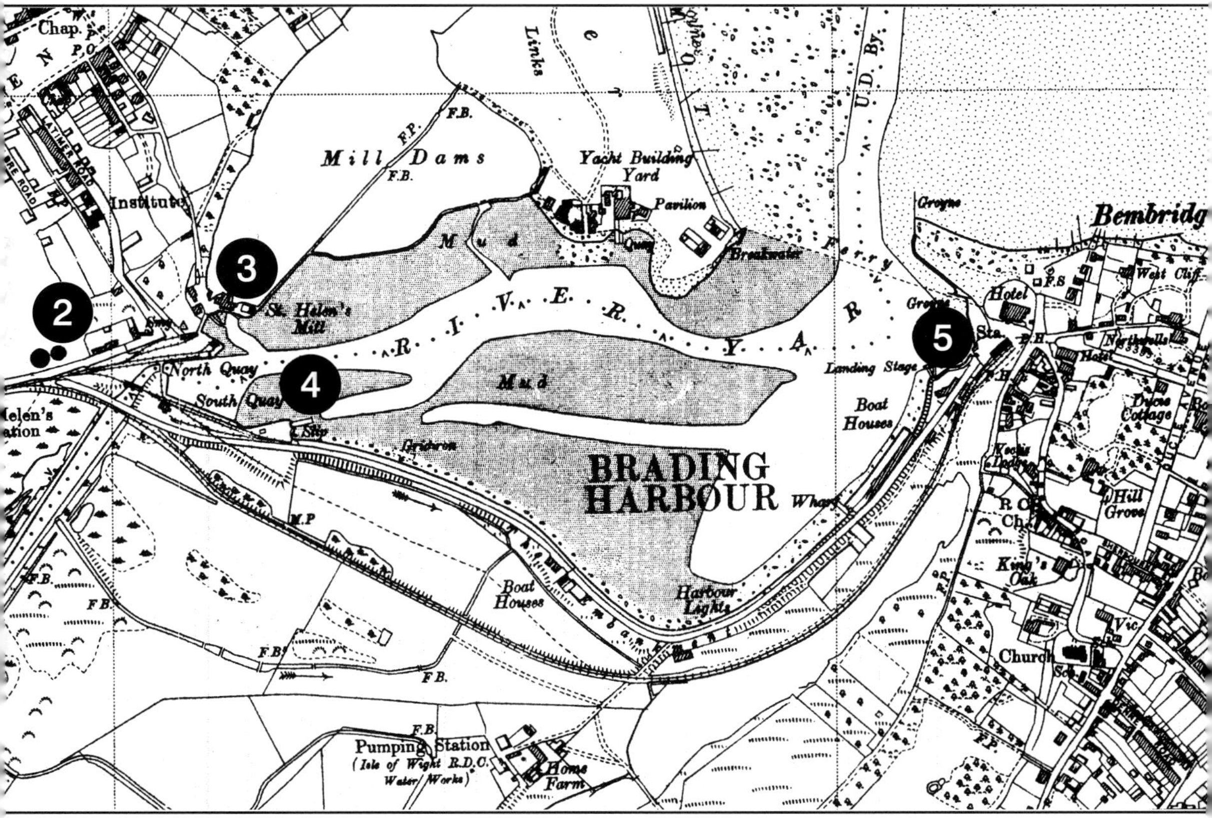

176. PS WHIPPINGHAM at Shanklin Pier

Although sent in 1945 it is likely that this delightful postcard image dates from the 1930s. The Southern Railway's largest and finest paddle steamers were *Whippingham* and *Southsea* both 825grt./1930. These two vessels were certificated to carry 1,050 persons each, and in view of their ability to manage a speed of 16kts they could venture away on the longer coastal excursions. Of course their capacity would also have made a huge difference on Summer Saturday services between Portsmouth, Southsea Piers, and Ryde. *Southsea's* career ended early as she became a casualty of WW2 Naval mine sweeping operations – a regular war time pursuit for shallow draughted paddlers. The coal fired *Whippingham* sailed on until economics and dwindling excursion tourist numbers ended her career in 1962. Shanklin Pier opened for business in 1891 but would not survive intact beyond the Great Storm of 1987. In the photograph *Whippingham* has probably already visited Sandown Pier with the next stop Ventnor, on a typical trip from Portsmouth and Southsea.

177. Unloading coal at Bonchurch 1861 →

Reproduced by the kind permission of the Isle of Wight Heritage Service is this fine colourful scene by T.M. Richardson, Jnr. of a bluff bowed little trading vessel at Horseshoe Bay. There is much of interest to be seen on the ship and the beach. Firstly, the ship would have been brought ashore very carefully to the sandy, rock-free part of the beach at high water. Kedge anchors would have been trailed out astern to aid ultimate hauling off and departure. To the left of the painting (starboard side of the ship), men, horses and carts are frantically removing the coal cargo, whilst simultaneously on the port side a separate gang of workers are loading beach sand as ballast for departure, by way of gang planks, ready for the high tide. Various local fishing craft are scattered about including a lugger and what appears to be a brand new boat. The overall image is exquisitely captured although the artist's treatment of the ship's rigging is a little difficult to determine. She looks most like a small brigantine or a topsail schooner of perhaps 70-100 tons carrying capacity. This ancient form of cargo discharge on a totally exposed beach would be largely carried out during the spring and summer months, well before the likelihood of autumn gales. There were of course disasters with such operations, yet some of these tough old ships and their fine seamen worked the coast for decades.

178. Ventnor in 1845 ↓

From an unknown artist's drawing c1845 here we see a largely undeveloped Ventnor looking from east to west. A small trading ketch has been brought ashore to work cargo on the beach. Ventnor's Gasworks was served with coal in this manner for decades. In the 1870s and 1880s a branch of the well known Wheeler family of longshoremen established a basic beach 'mini-port' where schooners, brigs and barges could load or unload their cargoes. The schooner '*Friends*' was reportedly a regular visitor.

179. Ventnor in 1861

This image is from another of the famous local Brannon family engravings. The detail and perspective achieved from such a high imaginary vantage point is incredible. It is just possible that the first pier of 1861 may have been that point – it shortly succumbed to the elements! A trading smack with horses and carts in attendance lays in a couple of feet of water out in the bay.

180. Ventnor Pier 1930s →

The final version of the pier opened in 1887 some twenty years after the railway came to Ventnor. Like its neighbours Sandown and Shanklin, it too would see many a visiting excursion paddle steamer. The first attempt by the Ventnor Pier and Harbour Company to build a pier had occurred in 1861, and another idea envisaged a harbour between two piers. Early attempts soon succumbed to the gales. However the 1887 structure managed to survive with its full length of 650ft from the shoreline until the fateful Great Storm of 1987.

181. Ventnor Haven construction →

In 2003 the *Ville* is just dropping another load of granite boulders to form the growing east side breakwater at Ventnor's new little harbour. Four hydraulically tilted hoppers are loaded by crane from the 'mothership' anchored out in the bay. Given the right tide and weather conditions the rocks can be offloaded quite precisely where required. Final positioning of the stone is by the orange painted tracked hydraulic crane almost awash in the incoming swell across the bay.

182. The end of the King's yacht

Dated July 8th 1936 and in strict accordance with the late King's final wishes, his beloved yacht *Britannia* 115reg.tons /1893 had been stripped of all fixtures and fittings. She was prepared for the tow to a position South of the Island to be scuttled. The famous cutter had been registered as owned by His Majesty King George V. A new replica *Britannia* is in 2012 fitting out at East Cowes. (See no.58 photograph)

183. The modern St. Catherine's Lighthouse

Trinity House started to construct a light tower on top of St. Catherine's Down in 1785 to warn shipping of the dangers below. It would never be completed as fog, mist and low cloud would have rendered it nigh on useless. In 1840, a new 120ft. tower near to the shoreline suffered the same problem until 1843, when reduced in height by 43ft. Electric lighting by generator replaced the oil lamp system in 1888. Lighthouses and lightships around England's shores are now remotely controlled and monitored by Trinity House from their main Harwich base with visiting technicians on maintenance work. Beyond, in the January 2012 photograph and despite it being a fine day, the notorious St. Catherine's Race is clearly visible. The ebb tide rushing over uneven ground around the Point causes overflows of broken water.

184. St. Catherine's Tower

Dating from the 1300s the original tower sits some 800ft above sea level. The story and reason for its construction has been told many times over the years. An oratory or chantry once stood roughly in line with the camera position in this image – abutting the octagonal built tower. A monk would keep the light (fire) burning to warn ships out in the Channel but the lofty perch and the fact that it stood well over one mile back from the sea did not render it of much use. Following Henry VIII's dissolution of the monasteries in the 1500s, no light was exhibited in any case for centuries! This area looks out over the true 'Back-of-the-Wight' with our starting point the Needles, distant.

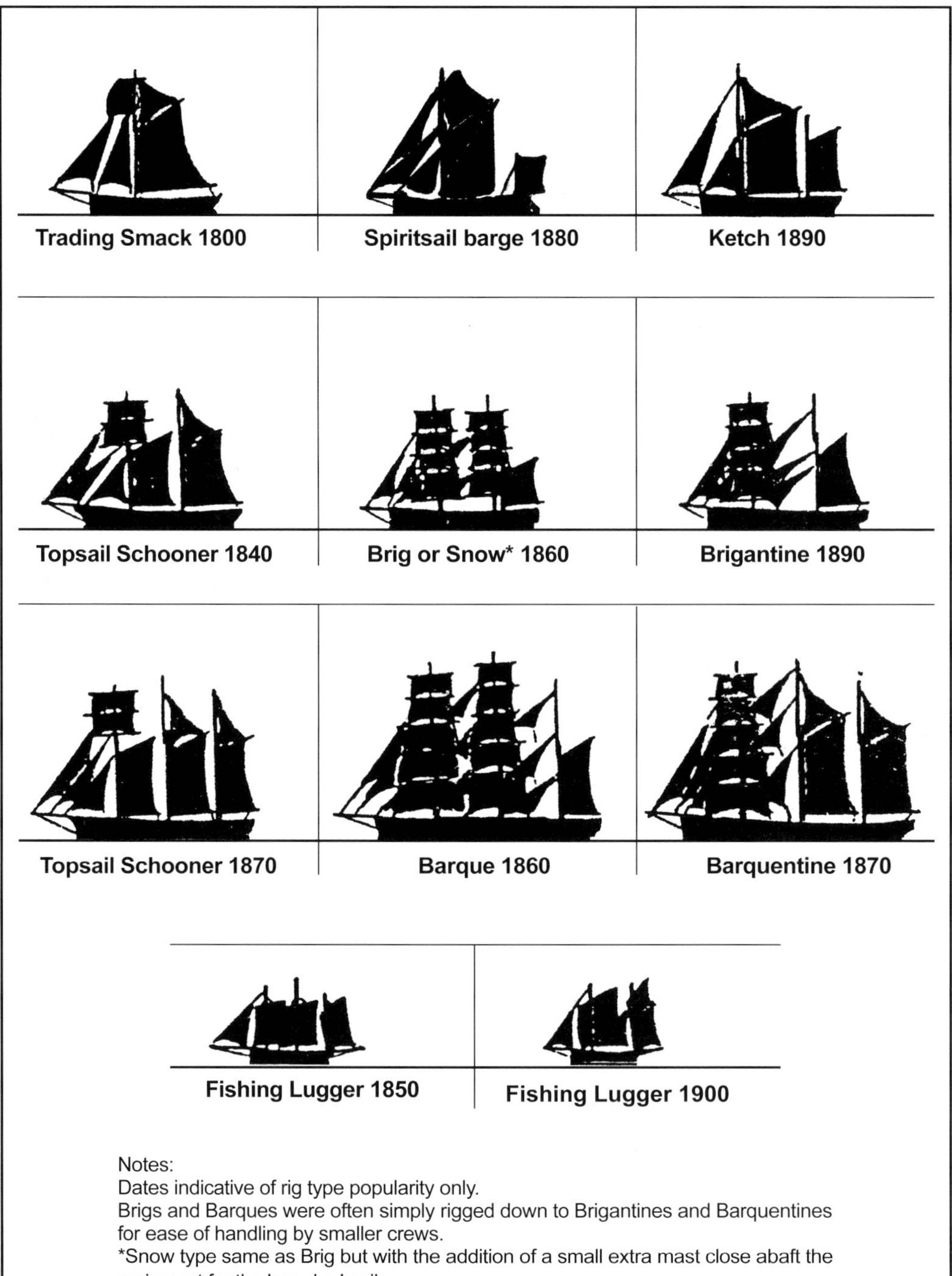
Trading Smack 1800
Spiritsail barge 1880
Ketch 1890
Topsail Schooner 1840
Brig or Snow* 1860
Brigantine 1890
Topsail Schooner 1870
Barque 1860
Barquentine 1870
Fishing Lugger 1850
Fishing Lugger 1900
Notes:
Dates indicative of rig type popularity only.
Brigs and Barques were often simply rigged down to Brigantines and Barquentines for ease of handling by smaller crews.
*Snow type same as Brig but with the addition of a small extra mast close abaft the mainmast for the 'spanker' sail.

'Trading vessel sailing rigs of the Solent – 1800-1900'

Bibliography

Ship Building from Smack to Frigate	Albion Publishing	1925	-
British Paddle Steamers	Geoffrey Body	1971	0 7153 5118 4
Isle of Wight Village Book	Federation of W.I.	1974	-
Island Longshoremen	Richard J. Hutchings	1975	-
Industrial Arch. in the IOW	Alan Insole & Alan Parker	1979	0 9063 2806 3
Steam Coasters & Short Sea Traders	Charles V. Waine	1980	0 9051 8404 1
The Ancient Town of Yarmouth	C.W.R.Winter	1981	0 9501 7797 0
Fifty fascinating facts about the IOW	John Dowling	1984	0 9509 3900 5
The IOW –An Illustrated History	Jack & Johanna Jones	1987	0 9461 5944 0
Isle of Wight at War	Adrian Searle	1989	0 9461 5958 0
Sealink Isle of Wight	John Hendy	1989	0 9513 0933 1
The Steam Collier Fleets	J.A.MacRea & C.V.Waine	1990	0 9051 8412 2
Maritime Heritage White's of Cowes	David L.Williams	1993	0 8579 4011 3
Put out the Flag	Derek Sprake	1993	1 8732 9500 6
Yarmouth – A Pictorial History	Geoffrey Cotton & Terry Kelsey	1995	0 9518 7231 1
Red Funnel. A Pictorial History	Michael Archbold	1997	-
The Book of the Solent	Maldwin Drummond & Robin G.McInnes	2001	0 9012 8130 1
Island Line	Ralph C.Humphries	2003	1 8993 9225 4
The Saunders-Roe Princess Flying Boat Project	Bob Wealthy	2003	-
Final Years of IOW Steam	Tony Molyneau & Kevin Robinson	2007	0 7110 3241 6
A History of Newport Quay & the River Medina	Bill Shepard & Brian Greening	2008	-

INDEX

(Ship and boat names are in capitals, with place names in lower case)

Acknowledgements

I would like to record my thanks and appreciation to all the kind individuals, societies and organisations who with their time, information and material have so helped with the compilation of this book, in particular: Stephanie Bagnall, Christine and Peter Bentley, Sarah Burdett, John Fletcher, Brian Greening, John Graves, Ken Hicks, John Horne, Robin G. McInnes O.B.E., Doreen and Jim Miller, Michael Millidge, Phil Neumann, Roger Silsbury, Richard Smout, and Christine Yendall.

Photographic Sources

Beken of Cowes 31; Brannon Collection 6,53,145,179;
Carisbrooke Castle Museum Trust 1,107,151,171;
East Cowes Heritage Centre 49,54;
Fotoflite 51,77,78,79,90,97;
Isle of Wight County Record Office 45,147;
Isle of Wight Heritage Service 143,177;
Isle of Wight Steam Railway 48, 172;
Michael Millidge 105;
West Cowes Heritage Society 34,35,47,56;
World Ship Society 5,50,52.

Easebourne Lane, Midhurst, West Sussex. GU29 9AZ
Telephone: 01730 813169 Fax: 01730 812601
Email: info@middletonpress.co.uk www.middletonpress.co.uk

Michael Langley

Solent - Creeks, Craft & Cargoes
South West Harbours - Ships & Trades
Sussex Beach Trades - Sea Coal to Trippers
Sussex Shipping - Sail, Steam & Motor
Trident Tankers Ltd - A Change of Course
Kent Seaways - Hoys to Hovercraft

Isle of Wight
RAILWAY ALBUMS

Branch Lines to Newport
Hampshire Narrow Gauge
including Isle of Wight
Isle of Wight Lines - 50 years of change
Ryde to Ventnor
Steaming Through the Isle of Wight

please see - www.middletonpress.co.uk for further details
or contact us for a brochure listing over 500 titles covering
Local History, Railway, Tramway, Trolleybus and Military topics.